HUMANITY

ROCKS /ARS

♡ Cindy

May the extraordinary stories of fabulous ordinary people inspire you to conquer your destiny. Enjoy the read.

Tiffany Hannett
July 2018

Cindy Rochstein

Humanitarian Rockstars
© Cindy Rochstein 2018

National Library of Australia Cataloguing-in-Publication entry (pbk)

Author:	Rochstein, Cindy, author.
Title:	Humanitarian Rockstars / Cindy Rochstein
ISBN:	978-1-925680-98-0 (paperback)
	978-1-925680-97-3 (ebook)
Subjects:	Non-Fiction – Charity -- Humanitarian
	Charity -- Children -- Pencils

Published by Cindy Rochstein and Ocean Reeve Publishing
www.pencilscommunity.com
www.oceanreeve.com

REEVE
PUBLISHING

contents

Preface

In *Humanitarian Rockstars* we take you behind the scenes to see what it's *really* like to run a successful charity. A free backstage pass to 'our kind' of rock concerts, a no-holds-barred approach to see the reality of what everyday humans, in fact humanitarians, do and achieve, in order to deserve the title, '*rockstar*'.

Why the title, '*Humanitarian Rockstars*'? It's such a juxtaposition of words. Many humanitarians would hesitate to call themselves 'humanitarians'. I think they believe it gives them grandeurs of titles that are irrelevant. I am learning that most people in this space of pure and authentic giving shy away from the spotlight and are often personally quite humble about their contributions. They get on with their purpose and work and have their heads down, only seeking attention to forward their causes.

The title of this book came from a discussion with Bela from OrphFund around the stereotypical well-meaning but misguided 'voluntourist'. The kind that do some good, but also do a whole lot of instagramming of themselves surrounded by cute orphans with the hashtags #savingorphans #savingtheworld #iamahumanitarian which ultimately cheapens the causes associated.

So, despite Bela's protests I decided it was time to reclaim the word 'humanitarian'. I see all these hardworking people as important and deserving of attention as rockstars, and so the title of this book was born. These amazing individuals are the real change makers of our time because they are saving people's lives and changing lives for the better. They are regular people with huge beautiful hearts who simply care and know their purpose. They are those same human beings that you walk past in the supermarket and do not notice, who achieve greatness, quietly. They are humbled in their service to others.

'**Humanitarian Rockstars**' takes you behind the scenes of a social enterprise, examining what really goes on inside a charity - revealing all the good bits and the bad bits. People don't want to read about organisations and strategy, they want to read about real people, about hope and inspiration and about making a difference. This story will take you on a journey meeting the people that are the heart and soul of the organisation, all the while showing you the 'truth', and how you too, can be involved and help change the lives of thousands.

Do you think you have what it takes to be a Humanitarian Rockstar? I think you might surprise yourself. If you want to learn more, then grab your backstage VIP pass and come inside and see a world of love, heart, and pure humility in all its forms. Learn how you can easily become a humanitarian and even get your family, kids, and workplace involved too! **Pencils Community** came from humble beginnings and a simple creative idea...**see how lives were changed and where it all began with just one flippin' pencil!**

Foreword by Ocean Reeve

We write for various reasons; build awareness; to discover meaning; to be fully alive; to make a difference – just to name a few. There is no more profound way to establish a legacy than through the written word and when our stories have an impact on millions, then our footprint on this world is firmly established. *Humanitarian Rockstars* is one such publication that establishes this legacy, not just for the author, but also because of the potential impact it will have on us as a community.

In a tech driven world, the story of Pencils Community offers a grounded and altruistic insight into the harsh realities many on our planet are living with daily. Some of the children impacted by this charity don't even know what a mobile phone is, let alone have the luxury of a pencil. I personally find as an ambassador to this amazing organisation and a leader in creative expression, that Pencils Community connects my two worlds with awesome synergy.

Humanitarian is a word that shouldn't really exist. The fact it does identifies that as a global community we have not succeeded in creating a word where each life is not equally valued. The need to have humanitarians in this world is a sad reality that we have a lot of work to do. What it has created is a group of individuals and organisations that are vocal and proactive in ensuring we take steps every day to a common goal – unity, equality, safety and peace. I commend all those that spend their waking hours making such a profound impact and I'm grateful that I have been asked to write the foreword for a publication that aligns with that purpose.

Now, the author…what can I say about Cindy Rochstein? Aka 'Rockstar'; aka 'Wonder Woman'. Well, she truly is Wonder Woman. After working with her in publishing all five of her books (and more to come), it is truly satisfying to see her skills and talent as a writer continue to grow and develop to the awesome standard she is now at. Reading this book has been a delight as Cindy has easily created that visual picture of what it means to be a *Humanitarian Rockstar*. Funny, raw, emotive and passionate are the words I would use to describe this amazing read.

My relationship with Wonder Woman has covered so many facets of the creative industry from writing and publishing, event management and pr, web design and social media, and we have shared the stage on numerous occasions. We have both worked for each other and also for the same company, but it is our friendship that transcends all of this. As you're about to read, Cindy has resilience like no other. Her 'no excuses' philosophy in life is an inspiration to all and I am always in awe of her drive and commitment to make the lives of others more fulfilling, often at the expense of her own well-being. When the superhero fad took off amongst our close network, it wasn't difficult to identify who Cindy resonates with and I am sure that when you finish reading *Humanitarian Rockstars* you will no doubt agree that she is truly a 'Wonder Woman'.

Cindy optimises the word 'humanitarian' as there is absolutely no ego, accolade or personal gain she collects from running Pencils Community; it is all for the love of humankind and a willingness to create as many joyful experiences for others that she can. Cindy optimises the word 'rockstar' in everything she does. Like a lead singer in a band, she captivates, engages and entertains an audience; the community; the world. When Cindy speaks it is not just a presentation. It is a reality check and one that will inspire and connect without fail.

In this book, Cindy identifies the reasons behind why she does what she does, along with supporting stories of others that live this inspired life. I am incredibly proud that my friend, my adopted sister, my colleague, breathes this magic every single day. So with that, I invite you all to experience the amazing story that is *Humanitarian Rockstars* and I hope she ignites that desire within you to reach out and make a difference.

Ocean Reeve aka Superman
Publisher/Inspirational Speaker/Mentor/ Creative
www.oceanreeve.com
www.emagineacademy.com
www.bookpublishingqueensland.com.au

I want to leave my footprints on the sand of time
Know there was something that,
something that I left behind
When I leave this world, I'll leave no regrets
Leave something to remember, so they won't forget
I was here, I lived, I loved, I was here
I did, I've done, everything that I wanted
And it was more than I thought it would be
I will leave my mark, soul, everyone will know,
I was here

~Beyoncé

Dear Cindy, I hope this has reached you safely. I have been inundated with pencils, unfortunately more coloured ones than black – but I didn't turn them down. Hope they will be useful. I do quite a bit of work, mainly knitting for charity. Good Luck with yours.

Regards, Shirley H.

CHAPTER 1

It's just a flippin' pencil

Get me off this bloody stage! I think to myself as I reach the end of my presentation and show my final slide. My feet feel like I am walking on dry ice – you know, the stuff that is so cold that it creates smoke on stage but if you touch it, it burns you. The level of pain shooting up to my knees, hips and spine is so bad that I could swear an invisible evil critter is slowly hitting me with a cricket bat. Whack! I step forward to place the microphone onto the lectern. Whack! Again, as I step to place my feet together.

As the audience rise out of their seats to clap, I can feel my smile widen. It's always there, my smile that is. Ever present. It's the only way to carry on through this agonising rollercoaster of suffering. If I let the smile go, "my disease" wins. I know that the tough times never last, but tough people always do. My heart pounds against my rib cage and I am happy and proud of myself for speaking today.

From my high vantage point onstage, the grand ballroom is filled with a mix of creative and corporate people. Most of them seated for the speaker's presentations but all of them arranged into stalls, with colourful display stands. They are advertising their businesses, their services or their creative pursuits.

1

I am presenting at a Gold Coast speaking event that is supposed to be a celebration and mix of the business world and creative world coming together. Yet, right now, the divide feels bigger than it's ever been.

This is supposed to be a joint venture, a coming together of two important, yet uniquely different groups in society. Creative people, with their intricate and ideas-way of thinking, who need more business skills if they are to succeed in marketing and selling themselves and their work. Equally, business leaders need more creativity in the work place, otherwise work places get ruled with iron fists.

Instead of this beautiful merging and free-flowing of ideas, the space feels full of intimidation, hungry competition, and aggression, as the event organisers (very business-oriented people) try to throw their weight around and control the creatives in the room.

With business and political agendas in mind, and ex-Prime Ministers present, the organisers are cold and ruthless in ensuring that their business objectives come first. In their closed-minded approach they miss the entire point of the event, and unfortunately, the art of creativity falls on deaf ears.

As far as stereotypes went, these men and women fit it to a tee – the business and corporate world – focus on the objective with little to no flexibility or open-mindedness from them, nor any meaningful connection between any of them. Ironic don't you think for a networking event?

As the clapping sound rings in my ears, my eyes blur and the faces disappear a little. I wonder how much of my exhaustion is from the two days of travelling prior just to be here. It was one hell of a car trip from Melbourne to Brisbane driving through outback New South Wales.

A week prior, I had come up with the bright idea to drive from Melbourne to Queensland, flights were expensive due to school holidays and I was in need of an adventure. Allocating two days, I estimated about eleven hours of driving per day. It would give me time to go over the presentation and get prepared for the days ahead, and besides, road trips are always fun! It also felt like a great 'timeout' from the sick and stressful few months leading up to this event.

Arriving late the night before the event, left no time to adapt to the unusually hot and humid weather, typical of the Gold Coast. I found the morning of the presentation stifling, and I sweltered under the conditions. The ballroom also lacked air conditioning, or rather, until the organisers decided to put it on. For business-minded people, they certainly showed limited events management experience.

Having spent years as an events and public relations manager in Europe, I know my skill set, and air conditioning and room temperature is one of the biggest considerations to be made when running an event. Your attendees must always feel good if you want them to stay, participate, and get the most out of whatever experience it is they are attending.

By the time the organisers realise their error and turn on the air conditioning, it was already too late. Men stood in sweat-soaked business shirts, and women patted down their makeup and wiped sweat off their foreheads.

I wasn't sure if it was the overall stress of the event, or the pain I felt, or the smell of human sweat that made me feel sick, but I knew that if I didn't get off this stage soon, the nausea train would kick in, and I would certainly regret such a public moment. The faint smell of mangos from Jen Compton's table filtered through the other smells and I clung onto that smell for dear life, breathing it in.

I use whatever reserves of energy I have left to draw on and walk as slowly down the steps of the stage as I can. Each step agonisingly pulling at my heart, every moment of every fibre in my brain wishing that this pain would go away and that my story was different. But it wasn't and as I step down one by one, the shooting ice picks from this 'magic madman' slice through every tendon and hit their intended target, my joints, each and every one of them.

Did you know that in your feet alone there are fifty-two bones, thirty-three joints, one hundred and seven ligaments, nineteen muscles, and some tendons that hold everything together? Right now, I can feel them all, and not just my feet. Ankles, knees, hips, back, shoulders, neck, elbows, wrists, and fingers. A symphony of pain. Still, I think, at least my internal organs are holding in there, for now.

All eyes watch my exit, stage left, as I make my slow way down several steps off stage and past the audience, moving back towards my seat. I won't lie to you, this is one of the hardest experiences to do, public speaking while in pain and keeping a happy face 'on' the whole time.

My high heels click on the wooden floorboards as I walk and even though they were carefully selected for today with their extra cushioning, they are as cruel as ever. I can't wait to get them off and switch back into my regular ballet flats that await me under my table at my stall. I smile as serenely as I can as I try to saunter through and pass a myriad of faces.

I have become used to the stares of sympathy and 'sorry for me' expressions in their eyes as I skim the audience and acknowledge that they are hearing my personal story for the first time. Shocking to some and disbelieving to others, the victim stereotype seems met. I look for familiar faces in the audience. My mentor, Ocean Reeve, is there, smiling and nodding, arms crossed in his relaxed state and beaming with pride.

Ocean and I have been on the road for many years presenting together and he is like a brother to me. This is my first official interstate presentation for Pencils Community and while I am used to talking to schools and children all the time, and on many topics, this is a new space for me. Over the years, I have learnt from Ocean ways to talk to and engage an audience. I think for my first presentation I did okay. There is certainly room for a critique later on. Even though I fumbled through some parts of my video and story, on the whole it was a solid beginning and it certainly delivered the message that it needed to:

That no matter what challenges we are faced with in life, there are NO excuses. If you want to achieve something badly enough then YOU will find a way.

'One day or Day one, you decide.'

I told the audience my personal story, I relayed to them some of the pain as best as I could without scaring them, and I told them about my purpose and mission in life – to help as many children as I can through my beloved charity, Pencils Community. And that in truth… **one pencil can change the world.**

I glance over the room and see my other colleagues Dion Jensen and Karen Clarke, who are also approving of my talk and I feel happy that I have done my part. It is amazing to feel connected to my team here presenting today along with Ocean. I see Dion preparing to get on stage and I make my way down the aisle past the other exhibition stands to my table. As I sit down, I grab some painkillers, water, and a can of coke. Behind-the-scenes there is always health chaos and I am grateful I have made it through this presentation without too much drama and that I am finally on the other side of it.

I swallow the all-too-familiar pills and wash them down with a coke (a trick to make them work faster) and boy, do I really need them to work much faster now! I try not to focus on the pain and the feeling that my body and joints feels like they are slowly snapping and breaking.

'Hey great talk!' says Mike, a fellow exhibitor who arrives at my stand and he leans in with a warm smile and handshake. I smile back and nod my thanks, grateful that someone has spoken to me like a real person rather than someone who is seen as a 'sick' human being. He signals at his watch and motions that we will catch up later on in the day.

'Tihei Mauri Ora!' suddenly ripples through the audience. And I look around. Like a musical tone suddenly bursting out of an instrument and yet at the same time, sounding smooth and silky like soft poetry being read to you by a lover. The tone lingers and has a feeling of deep longing connected to it as the spirituality seems to spiral around the venue. It commands me and everyone else in the room to listen.

It's as if a king of the past strides onto the stage. Standing there is my friend, Dion Jensen, all 6'4" of him, his suit-clad body moulded by years of military and police service. He is an impressive figure. His islander origins and Samoan-born presence make him gentle, loving, and loyal to those in his family and friendship circle. Yet the audience sees a towering figure. A broad-shouldered man standing above them with an authoritative stance and no-nonsense nature, and you just know that you are about to hear something very special.

'Ko Ruapehu te maunga, Ko Hautapu te Awa, Ko Ngati Tumatauenga te iwi, Ko Dion Jensen ahau, Noa reira, Tēnā koutou, tēnā koutou, tēnā tatou katoa'

This time, the tone and words come from a much deeper place, a place of inner strength as Dion calls upon his ancestors. Although he is not Māori, this *'Mihi'* is learnt at kindergarten age and links him to his land and ancestors through his Army connection. Depending upon who he is talking to, *'Ngati Pirihimana'* can be added to for his police connection or if he speaks to corporates. Being Samoan, he can also do a Samoan version if he is with Pacific Islanders. He acknowledges his tribe, Ngati Tumatauenga, the God of War (Army) as he goes forward to claim the mountain (Mount Ruapehu) and river (Hautapu River) of the training area where he and his team all trained and learnt their skills needed for war.

He places the audience in somewhat of a trance. His spiritual calling and traditional and respectful welcome to the group silences the otherwise noisy room of over one hundred people. Dion Jensen introduces himself and honours the connection to his mountain, his river, his tribe, and himself. And while there were patches of silence in mine and Ocean's presentation, right now, you can hear a pin drop in the room.

'Hi, my name is Dion Jensen and I save lives. That's my purpose and today we are going talk about the monsters under the bed and how to make friends with them. Just like in Scooby-Doo, the monster is always unmasked and dealt with and isn't so scary in the end.'

He proceeds to floor the room with a powerful presentation concerning post-traumatic stress and the way it impacts; not just the lives of service people and their loved ones but for anyone who has experienced a stressful period in their life. He then does something that utterly shocked and intrigued me at the same time.

'As with the end of any military presentation, you honour the speakers who come before you.' And he proceeded to stretch out his arm and point his hand towards my good friend Ocean.

'There is a man who knows his purpose! He is a man that helps people bring their stories to life! He inspires passion and creativity for everybody willing to listen to him and yet there were people in this room talking while he was presenting.' Dion pauses and lets the statement sink in along with the bashful behaviour surely being felt by some right now.

His hand then moves to me.

'There is a woman who knows her purpose! She changes lives and helps children colour their world. And you heard her presentation…she should be dead!' The audience is hanging off his every word.

'She knows her purpose so strongly, that she comes to talk to you, every moment in pain, about a flippin' pencil that changes the world.

Why?

Because there is love behind it!

And some of you didn't even listen!' His eyes scan the room to demonstrate that he knows and sees everything with his heightened skills of situational awareness. He continues.

'You're lucky my friend Chris* was not here because he would have thrown chairs at you people who were talking and being so rude when Cindy and Ocean spoke.'

(*Chris being a respected soldier brought up to listen when people speak).

It's at this moment in the room that I can feel the love and respect from Dion and the unmistakable authority that he represents. I later learn, in historical reference, every woman has a life cycle: from maiden to mother to crone (wise woman). But that not every man goes from boy, to warrior, to sage. Some men are just boys until they die, some boys transition to warriors and protectors and never leave that space, but there are few that transcend to sage. A sage is someone with the experience, integrity, and ability to teach others and pass on life's lessons.

Ocean is a sage and Dion is a sage. They both have something to teach everybody and are sharing it now. Later on, once Dion finishes his presentation there will be a crowd four-people deep at his table, crying, connecting, and looking for love and help. Such is the power of this man... both men.

Sitting there at my table, surrounded by love and Pencils, in a stifling hot room, in a day that has exhausted all my energy and challenged my emotions is when I realise what I have done. The ah-haaa moment when you can see what you have created with supreme clarity. Hearing the story back through another's eyes – seeing yourself as they see you, and coming from a man of such humility, integrity, and respect – helps me truly see the magic of what I have created.

As I sit there in stunned epiphany, Dion's hand moves to Karen Clarke, the final speaker in our team. He gives her such an emotional introduction that it silences the room and brings them to tears. She walks on stage also in unashamed tears at the level of love and support shown to her by what I can only describe as a beautiful man. And it takes her some moments to speak. Karen is in the most vulnerable position and yet she is at her most powerful on stage in that moment. Raw, honest, authentic. She has long been my idol and mentor and I am beyond thrilled to be in the team with her to learn and grow.

The moment has me thinking about all those people I have met in my life, particularly those in my two-year journey as Founder of Pencils Community, who go unrecognised, who do this because they have found their purpose too, just like the four presenters here today, Ocean, Dion, Karen, and myself. These wonderful volunteers, all with their unique stories, working in Pencils Community or in some way connected to us, all of them humanitarians who know their purpose and their deeper question of 'WHY' they do what they do.

This book is for you.

Dear Cindy. Thank you for all the commitment and dedication you have put in for making our action possible!!!

Love from Jacinta,
Danae, and Amelia xx

CHAPTER 2
#canoefleet

'Where are these sugar canes I think to myself?' as the intermi-nable kilometres of New South Wales and a lack of tropical feeling scenery surrounds me.

It is twenty-four hours earlier and I am somewhere between that point of overtired and weary and know that the journey is not over yet. I am still a few hours from my destination.

Driving from Melbourne to Gold Coast, taking the route diago-nally across New South Wales has been tiring. Having failed short of my estimated eleven hours driving per day to get from Melbourne to Queensland in just two short days, I am left with fourteen hours of driving. As with any trip, the last few hours are the longest as I calculated that I had been driving through NSW for at least fifteen hours of the twenty-two-hour journey.

By the time I finally reach the mysterious sugar canes on the border of NSW and Qld, I am nearly at Ocean's house, the pace slowing with every minute of peak hour. Rolling in about 6pm, I am greeted with open arms by Ocean and his wife Vicki Jane, excited to see them in person after five months.

With just enough time to have a quick shower and drink before we hop back into the car to drive to dinner in Surfers Paradise. Dion and his sister Amanda, are staying at an apartment there while in town for the presentation. By the time we pull up we find our second wind, so we pile out of the car and head up to the apartment.

We are soon greeted with a tall, tattooed man with a warm smile and a generous heart. 'Come up bro!' says Dion as he squeezes Ocean with a hug. I love seeing men feel so comfortable that they can express closeness with one another. I am also greeted with the same warmth and we head on up to devour some pizza and drink wine.

As we all arrive we see Karen and her husband Wayne, have beaten us there. They are familiar faces, who I have met on many occasions. They, like Dion, and myself have been a part of Ocean's publishing journey for a long time.

Ocean is the one that connects us all and in his devious and cunning mind has brought us all here tonight for a reason, unknown to all of us. The creative connector we like to call him, or as he is commonly referred to as 'Superman!'

Over pizza we make conversation about the meaning of tattoos and we discuss our books. We are in a high-rise apartment that is common for Surfers Paradise and we are sitting around in a circle in the lounge room. The silk curtains blow in and out of the sliding door as the night is thick with humidity. From that height we could have seen a gorgeous view. Only our attention is elsewhere.

'So, Cindy…why don't you begin with your story?' Ocean asks me with a secretive smile.

'Really?' I say, rolling my eyes, 'Doesn't everyone here already know it?'

He shakes his head in true Ocean fashion and looks at me. I know that look. It means, there is a point to this, I am asking you to speak your truth.

As with every time I begin my personal story, I gloss over it quickly with some facts. To me it's been over twenty years of suffering and it's difficult to explain to people what it's like to live in chronic pain. I mean they can all walk upstairs and not think twice, unlike me.

Ocean urges me to go into more detail, so I begin by asking the group, 'Can you in fact love a shark?'

I continue.

They are bemused and intrigued.

'I wasn't always like this you know. Before I was nineteen years old I was fit and healthy, or so I thought. I excelled at gymnastics and trained since the age of five. I was also good at most sports in general, particularly swimming, spring board diving, dancing, and athletics. I was smart too, and went on to study Earth Sciences at university, in other words, Geology & Planets. It wasn't until I was nineteen years old and travelled on my own for the first time that life would change forever for me, only not in the way I expected.

I was at the end of my first year of university and had met some wonderful and influential friends, I felt invincible and I felt strong, I was ready to discover the world and travel on my own. I thought I knew everything. None of my friends had the means to fly to Vietnam, but I had worked part time as a gymnastics coach for the last four years, so I thought, 'Well I'll go anyway!' So, I packed my backpack and made my way through International Departures at Melbourne's Tullamarine Airport.

Only nineteen when I left for my life-changing trip to Vietnam - I wanted to see and experience the world, challenge myself, and immerse myself in a culture both exotic and beautiful. This was also a time when it wasn't 'cool' to travel to countries like this, with a more safe and traditional path being England or Europe on a Contiki tour. But as you will soon learn, I never do anything by the rulebook and so, I set off on my epic journey to conquer the path less travelled.

Vietnam is a country of amazing beauty, yet, riddled with a dark history. The fallout, like land mines, the lingering presence of Agent

Orange, and extreme poverty are the scars that juxtapose against the beauty of the land and its people. I had set out to conquer and change the world in typical nineteen -year-old ego style…the only thing was… it changed me.

At first the trip changed me, for the better - I learnt to travel independently, learn some language and culture, gained self-confidence, all those wonderful attributes when you succeed at a personal goal. I felt enriched in the PEISES of life (what I refer to as Physical, Emotional, Intellectual, Social, Environmental, and Spiritual aspects). In my opinion, our lives are made up of PEISES, but we need to look at them as a whole, to look at ourselves holistically and not compartmentalise in order to achieve wellness and be our best. Ironically, writing about wellness is also something I do now.

The Latin definition and interpretation of PEISES is 'Balance' and my definition reflects this also. For instance, you could be an ultra-fit marathon runner, and yet be completely void of any spiritual awareness. You may be wealthy with a big house, and yet feel unsatisfied and emotionally closed. Or you might be physically disabled, and yet still emotionally and mentally strong, like me.

However, travelling in Vietnam proved to have one downside. In fact, it was such a massive downside that it could have cost me my life. It wasn't a tsunami or a typhoon, nor was it a snake bite or something as big and dramatic as that. It was in fact so tiny, that it would have been nearly invisible to the naked eye. Literally, it was part of the micro-cosmos.

A tiny tick, carrying a disease by the name of Rickettsia, bit me. We now believe it was a cluster of bites on the back of my right leg, but I didn't even notice until I was back in Australia, and I certainly did not know, the importance of a bunch of tiny red marks on my leg. There were no ticks embedded in my leg, just red marks that looked like small bites of some kind. The size of half a five-cent coin – not even noticeable, the kind you would get sitting outside at night camping in Australia. In that moment though, life was about to take a dramatic downward spiral.

Upon my return to Melbourne, I seemed ok, but I knew intrinsically I had changed. Something felt wrong. I had lost a lot of weight quickly on the trip and put it down to my vegetarian diet and not eating that much while travelling as well as a lot of hiking. Over the next few years, I suffered unusual symptoms out of the blue. Extreme jaundice, rashes on my torso, swollen joints and injuries to my knees and wrists that couldn't be explained. I would wake up and it would look like my knee had dislocated in my sleep, or that I was partially paralysed temporarily, unable to walk, get dressed properly, or hold a cup of coffee.

Twelve long years passed, multiple surgeries and countless tests, dressed in a simple hospital robe feeling alone and vulnerable, while doctors looked for a reason. I didn't feel like anything that my younger nineteen year old felt – I didn't feel strong or invincible any more. I felt weak, tired, and sore and out of control. I was constantly told there were no answers and there was nothing that could be done.

Finally, after more than a decade, a surgeon noticed my rash and a quick excursion to the Alfred Infectious Diseases Unit led to a diagnosis of 'Rickettsia' which finally came through on the hundreds of blood tests. (*For those not familiar with Rickettsia, it is similar in many ways to Lyme's disease*). The unique part of Rickettsia is the cumulative effect it has over time. You know that joke about the person that goes to the doctor and the doctor says I have good news…we're going to name a disease after you? After twelve years, I had a toxicity level high enough to make me extremely sick. And its discovery made my very serious doctor jump up and down and shout

'You beauty! We found it.'

It was a blessing and a curse all in one. No-one has ever had this disease untreated before, for twelves years, and survived.

I was treated with a triple course of Doxycycline, the same medicine used for anti-malarial drugs for when you travel. Since 'my cure' of the disease, I have continued to suffer physically. Like Vietnam, my body has scars and lingering effects. Scars to everybody else and yet they are the demons I have had to fight off mentally at 3am and win.

'You seem to have developed an auto-immune disease from the tick bite' said the chorus of medical professionals.

'Only we don't know what it is, perhaps a reactive arthritis'.

Crutches and bandages, from swollen joints and limited range of movement, were to become a regular part of my day, as were the painkillers and the next round of whatever immunosuppressant drugs my doctors wanted to try me on. I went along with them, they are doctors right, they know what to do when you are sick, right? Only they had no answers for me, just treated the symptoms as they occurred. There is no cure.

I like to laugh about it sometimes and have renamed my disease, 'the shark disease.' As long as I keep moving, and keep swimming like a shark, I won't die. When I move I am not as stiff and sore as when I am still. When I do stop or sit, or at night time, I can hardly move, I can't turn over in bed and if the blankets slip off I have to lie there in the cold unable to move my body the way it's meant to, even just to pull a doona on me is impossible. The pain can be all-consuming if you let it.

I am now forty-two – for over half my life I have been in a state of chronic physical pain and have been a pincushion for every medical treatment available, forever the lab rat for medical staff to experiment with. I've become so conditioned to doctor's appointments and injections that I don't even think that they are anything other than 'my normal'. The doctors love letting the student doctors and nurses administer blood tests to me, because their learning mistakes don't even register on my pain scale.

Last month's medical specialist statement was, 'I know you are looking for answers, but we just don't have the technology yet to know how to treat you properly, and we do not know how much damage has been done to your body. No one has suffered this disease untreated for so long and survived. You are lucky that for now, it is just in your joints and not your internal organs. By all accounts, you shouldn't be here!'

Now, I don't know about you, but it takes some tough-ass mental fortitude to be gracious in hearing a statement like this, that this is my physical fate. I never knew I could string so many swear words together in my head. Yet externally gracious and accepting, does not mean I have given up. Acceptance is not defeat, it is not giving up, it is acknowledgement of something I have little control over.

I will always look for ways to improve my health, and ways to address all my PEISES, even if my physical one is often challenged. Walking to the end of my street may not seem like much to some but to me it is a big deal and something I am so grateful of. So yes, I will admit to telling you all now, that I have in fact, become a shark. A sense of humour is often required!

I like to think that over the years I have got pretty good at it. I have learnt to separate my physical from my other PEISES (even though I work daily on my physical). I try to find the inner balance of life; a wonderful combination of Eastern and Western medicines.

I tell the group that I am about to embark on round 982 million of new treatments. With the next drug treatment via self-injection, government approved experimental drugs known as Biologics. This means that every other high-class side effect drug hasn't worked, not the cortisone and not the chemo. I am going to combine my new ritual with golden turmeric paste, vegetable broth, meditation, swims in the hydro-pool, green kale breakfast shakes, and a newly researched nutmeg drink to help me sleep. Yummy…Hmmm this cocktail in general is debatable, but food is medicine, right?

However, despite all the drama, my mind-set, and my emotional and mental health are strong. I am happy, and I love my life. I have a beautiful daughter and an extended growing family and all I could wish for. I have my physical challenges, but I will not let them stop me. Sharks cannot stay still, so rather than *let* this mysterious disease control me, I control it.

One way in which I do this is through my beloved charity, Pencils Community, which as you all know is what I am up here in Queensland to talk about. I feel honoured that Pencils Community has helped thousands across many countries and continues to do so. It is these feelings that keep me building and growing Pencils Community and helping get pencils to those in need.

It's what gets me out of bed in the morning and moving every day, applying my bandages, taking my painkillers, and getting on with life. 'I would rather wear out than rust out,' says my Mum as she keeps me focused on the tough days.

I look around the room at the quiet faces and say quietly but with dignity, 'I am not just the girl who went to beautiful Vietnam and came back with an illness, I am so much more than that. At least I am a shark, and even sharks can love and deserve to be loved.'

I take a sip of my wine and look at Ocean. He has his normal facial expression but there is an air of compassion to it. He has known my story from the beginning. It's the others who look at me now with warmth. They are in disbelief, but they don't look at me with pity. They look at me with love. And in that moment, I feel like I have been swept up into a loving embrace filled with a purity few experience.

The night unfolds and the stories from each of us come out. Each person takes time to go through their life-changing moments and dramatic events. Stories of robbery, alienation from family, illness, war, regret, violence, and more. Insights and mistakes.

At times throughout the evening, we hold hands, give hugs, and toast drinks in respect; tears and laughter are ever present. It is disarming in many ways to be in a group of new colleagues who now feel like family. Each knowing what the other has been exposed to or forced to endure. We each feel vulnerable; our stories, our thoughts, and feelings. It is a magical moment of serene acceptance and divine capability from everyone and it is one of the rawest emotional spaces I have ever been.

Clever, Ocean. I think to myself. He has just created an unbreakable bond and connection between us all. I am sure he didn't even know what would unfold as we all sequentially went around the circle. Perhaps he suspected, but I think he couldn't foresee that in that moment, bringing us together created the inner sanctum.

As the night takes a breather and conversations disperse into smaller groups, I sit on the seat next to Dion. He and I lament the same feeling of sadness of being alone in our individual purpose and pursuits. We liken it to a being in a metaphorical canoe, paddling through the waters of life and challenges alone. The rush of the wind as it sweeps up your almighty oars and swings through the water carving up the ocean. Yet the path in purpose alone can seem like you are canoeing into a headwind at times, as challenges arise and unfamiliar territory with no one around to help. No one to bounce ideas off or brainstorm…until now.

They say, every successful businessperson needs to have a 'Top 5' – a group of people that will guide you, critique you, mentor you, and more, as your business develops. Their support is a given, however, they won't placate your ego, as they are there to push you to your limits to help you grow and succeed to greater heights.

Dion and I go on to agree that after this evening of giving of each person's heart and story, we now feel like we are a group of canoes, sailing together. A fleet of canoes that join together and in doing so can now suddenly glide through the waters effortlessly rather than sailing head first into a strong wind. Strength in numbers.

We have become a canoe fleet. A force of knowledge and insight into our unique areas. Sages and Wise-women and all of us experts in our fields and coming together to deliver a stronger message. That we are in fact – changing lives by saving lives. We know our purpose and now we are a purpose united. We have become the #Canoefleet.

I hope this helps someone!

Love Jodie P and Family

CHAPTER 3

A Fireman, a Shower... An Idea

It is amazing what thinking of a fireman in the shower can accomplish. I turn the old brass taps and they squeal as they release thousands of water droplets at once. Instantly cold, then lukewarm and finally to hot in seconds. For an old beach-house, I am just thankful for having hot water. I wait for the chilled ceramic shower base to warm up before I step in.

Burning hot droplets wash over my shoulders and back, my hair darkening as the water saturates it. I reach for the soap first. My hands and arms are messy, and I am not wanting to touch my face with them. I slowly spin the soap in my hands until it makes a lather. The suds turn purple, then blue then pink as the ink mixes into them. Black texta marks and dirt ground into my fingernails slide off my skin and the shower base looks like a swirling technicolour art piece.

I tilt my head back until the water runs down over my face. My toes, that were first curled in the shower, are now stretched, as is every other muscle and tendon, relaxed and releasing the day's tension. As my eyes close under the weight of the water, the rhythmical sound of the shower permeates my eardrums and transcends me into a meditative state. Just like repeating a daily 'om' it is the act of saying YES to the universe accepting everything that life puts in front of you. This meditative water mantra seeps through my inner core and I can feel a crystal moment where my mind is clear.

I can see in my mind memories and images of children, laughing and giggling. Their worn, old clothing is barely a protective layer for their harsh climate and weather elements. The children are so truly happy, chatting away to each other, high-pitched sounds of joy, but they are not in English. They almost sound as if they are singing.

Smash! The sound of a cup dropping brings me out of this moment. My mind now in tatters from my beautiful vision of the children's happiness.

'Sorry, Mum!' I hear yelled from the kitchen. 'It's not broken!' comes the backup statement.

Broken cups are by-the-by when you have a six-year-old who is learning.

I try to relax again, desperate to get back to my peaceful moment. Images of the day flash like an old Polaroid camera. The cleaning, the mess, the trying to get on top of housework and a messy school desk. My image roller-deck stops on a fireman. 'Oh, how clichéd' I think to myself; a fireman in the shower, and I laugh at my own absurdity.

I recall seeing on Facebook images of my firemen friend, Grant. He posted photos of his trip last year to an orphanage in Vietnam in which he volunteered. He was going back again this year. Photos of half-finished buildings, children playing and learning in classrooms, garden projects, bandages, and children being fed.

I wonder if he would like that box of pencils? I think to myself. Only minutes ago, I was sorting through my daughter's desk. That led me to this shower, after being covered in dirt, glue, what look like dried ink, textas, and glitter. In each desk drawer was every imaginable colour and stationery item you could think of - rainbow gel pens, 'Smiggle' pencils, erasers in the shape of pineapples, sharpeners in the shape of penguins, 'Typo' exercise books, and enough rulers that I could measure the length of the entire house with.

It was September 2015, and our council had just announced its annual hard rubbish collection. For one week every year, broken couches and old tables were thrown out along with a mass of other household items that had seen their used-by date. Junk littered the streets and you slowly watched it disappear from neighbouring suburbs until it was your turn. *We are such a bunch of waste makers* I think every year. There is almost a sport in that if you can find an item that can still have a half-life, it is taken off the pile and placed inside your house. People are known for cruising the streets in their utes, loading up book cases, wardrobes, and weirdly enough old lawn mowers. I guess they want them for their parts? What's not picked up goes to landfill.

Spring-cleaning in the house motivated me to also downsize the furniture; clean up the rubbish and unused items that strangled our living space. I moved from room to room in the weeks prior and today found myself in the study. Before me was my daughter's very messy Grade One desk, covered in an array of stationery items. In typical six-year-old interior design, glitter dusted every surface, drawer, and was now heavily grouted into the floorboard gaps.

'How is it possible that we end up with our own personal newsagency?' I mumble under my breath, with the colourful items now filling a huge box. This was way more than what one child could ever use. One by one, the unused and discarded items are tossed into the box. In a matter of minutes, the box stands half filled, enough to fill six large shoeboxes of pencils, pens, crayons, and more.

I lug the heavy box downstairs. It is a precarious staircase at the best of times and I am sure not built to any building code. It is one of those peculiarities to this house, like the squealing shower, that over time you get so used to that you don't even notice any more.

I often refer to this house as the beach shack; it has the old qualities of a shack, located a stone's throw from the beach and in its day would have been grand. Over time, areas of the house were added on so that now it resembles a hotchpotch of now-enclosed garages and attached granny flats. Downstairs has its own kitchen and so it is almost a self-sufficient space if we were to have a boarder or someone live with us. Right now, it is called the roller-rama room and is a big empty space that holds our roller skates, hammock, and a plethora of hardly-used sporting equipment.

Upstairs is a typical three-bedroom setup with kitchen, bathroom, and lounge. We live upstairs, spending a great deal of time on the balcony, drinking wine, eating meals, and looking out in both directions to the sea and Mount Dandenong in the opposite direction. Around the other side of the house, a small balcony about five metres long runs down the side of the house, and in Spring and Summer time a beautiful grape vine grows through it. On hot days, underneath the balcony is the coolest place in the house and has fondly been named the 'Vineyard' to friends. It is also the best place to have a wine on a hot summer's night or dinner outside.

Hot, dirty and flustered, I drag the box down the remaining stairs and almost limp it out to the bin. I must look like the 'elephant man' to the neighbours. Thinking it would be better in the rubbish bin than on the nature strip, images flood though my mind of picking these pencils up again off the side of the road as the furniture rummagers go through them with their torches later at night. This convinces me that the bin is the place for them to go now.

I heave the box up onto my knee and balance it on the edge of the bin. It is surprisingly heavy. I am making lots of noise with the awkwardness of the box and my reduced physical capabilities from my latest swollen knee incident. I hope that my grunts scare away any of the big huntsman spiders that like to hang out under the lid. Being mid-September, we are coming up to what we termed in our Uni days as the 'electrical storm month'. October is when the lightning displays are frequent due to the new warmer weather as it develops for our Spring and Summer.

I flip the lid of the bin and to my luck, there are no creepy crawlies. I don't have a fear of spiders; being a single mum, you don't really have much choice when you have a huntsman lowering itself into the Christmas presents and a screaming four-year-old.

As the box teeters on the edge, something stops me. Call it divine intervention, say it was the angels or the universe, but in that moment, I say out loud, 'I just can't do this, it's such a waste'.

Grant welcomed my call regarding the pencils and said he would check with his friend Tiffany who was organising the Vietnam contingent. For years, she had been going backwards and forward to this orphanage after a life-changing trip to Vietnam altered her path, just like me. Vietnam has a habit of getting under your skin. Seeing the poverty in the school and orphanage that is run by nuns, Tiffany set out over the years to help them, supporting with educational items, building repairs, and maintenance, firewood deposits (in order to cook meals), gardens for food, and other items such as vitamins and minerals, lice treatments, first aid, band aids, and bandages.

Grant was a regular on these trips and every September, groups of volunteers would travel over for a month and be delegated jobs to assist. The children loved the yearly visits and many volunteers formed a part of their schooling, playing games, singing, and general wellbeing. Knowing this, I decided to make the one decision that would turn this idea from just an idea into a light-bulb moment.

I put out a message on Facebook to my friends, attached with a picture of the box of pencils I had tidied from my daughter's desk. It read:

'Hey, don't throw out your pencils and pens on hard rubbish, I have a home for them all. Get in touch with me or just drop them off at my front door.'

This one message, not especially well written, is the message that began our charity as we know it today - Pencils Community.

Little did I know that an abundance of boxes would turn up at my door daily. There would be pencils put into my mailbox, the mums at school would greet me at pick up time with a box of pencils and so a chain reaction had begun.

I decided that if I emailed a few local schools, they too might want someone to give their unused items to at the end of the school year. I know our local schools are big on sustainability and I thought the teachers would appreciate tidy classrooms as the end of the school year approached.

I sent out seventeen emails to local schools and I had 100% uptake. The schools **loved** the idea. My friend's son, Hugo drew a picture that became our first logo and his mum, Monique and I visited the schools and collected boxes. That year (2015), I spoke at one school assembly about donating pencils, and my daughter and school friends spoke at their school assembly. The part that excited me the most was not only the waste minimisation, but that our children could get involved from any age, from the five-year-old that handed over a handful of her favourite pencils to the twelve-year-olds that organised the collection as part of their school captain duties. An evolution of junior humanitarians had begun.

As the collection of donated pencils arrived and the boxes and piles grew, the downstairs roller-rama room slowly began to fill up. We were too late in the year to get our pencils on that first Vietnam trip but would be able to help them the following year along with an additional collection of bandages.

The very first place we were able to send our pencils was East Timor, it was November 2015. A container ship filled with clothing and essential items was sent over annually to a man who worked in the capital, Dili. His mum organised the container ship each year once she heard of the poverty and primitive living conditions. She wanted to help, and this was a way in which she could help her son and the people of East Timor. A contact of Monique's knew of this container and she was over the moon that we were able to assist. In a matter of days, we packed up the pencils, pencil cases, and stationery and delivered them to their intended destination, the 'Mum'.

It's funny when you look at the power of mums – they have a unique way of just getting things done. They act now and question later. They use the power of the 'Mum Mafia' – they spread the word, talk in playgrounds and cafes, and share on Facebook. They are the drivers of huge business and I think would make the best spies ever – seemingly to appear they are just talking kids or school stuff over lattes! They were and *are* pivotal in the movement of Pencils Community.

Looking back this was a big realisation for me. I knew the power of women before, but I hadn't seen it in action like this. I now knew the 'what' and the 'how' to moving pencils around. I knew that it took some small logistical planning and some action but that it didn't seem too hard. It wasn't rocket science; it was a case of, 'Here we have loads of stuff we don't use, and you guys have none, would you like it?' Pencils Community was always intended as a gift to those in need, and to this day that is still the core of what we achieve.

It was time to formulate a much bigger plan.

Dear Pencils Community, thank you for doing such a wonderful thing for the world's children.

Kellie S.

CHAPTER 4
Bela (OrphFund)

The phone rings. It's nearly midnight. On the other end of the line I hear a woman's voice introducing herself as Bela. I know her by name as she has been in touch via Facebook Messenger requesting some donations of pencils and school supplies for some kids in Africa for a charity that she volunteers with called, OrphFund.

She's calling from a work trip in London to sort out what has become a bit of a mess. In time she will become my absolute idol and the first person to teach me what the real concept of being a 'humanitarian rockstar' is all about.

'Okay so let's figure this out,' she says reassuringly. Having been a part of massive projects before such as container ships, she is aware and patient that this is my first time and I am somewhat of a 'newbie'.

I am exhausted and frustrated. We have been packing pencil cases for over fifteen hours today and the previous days also. Downstairs in the back room we have laid out shoeboxes and ice cream containers and sorted all the pencils into colours, doing the same for textas. Separate piles for erasers, rulers, and sharpeners. Our production line is set up. All ready to go into a mysterious shipping container that I cannot seem to get a straight answer of how to get our pencils into.

'Okay, where are we up to?' Bela says in a calm but assertive tone. I like her already, particularly her no bullshit approach.

'Oh Bela,' I sigh, dramatically. 'We have packed thousands of pencils into pencil cases along with all the other items. They look amazing and we are just coordinating a drop-off or collection with your Melbourne team who aren't making the most sense to me, something about leaving the boxes on the side of the road and then to be picked up later?' I say with worry about the thought of leaving all our hard work sitting on the side of the road.

Perhaps I am too overtired to work out what the logistics are or am feeling so incredibly out of my depth.

Bela starts to smooth things over, she knows it's just a miscommunication. She can tell that I am tired but reassures me that we are all working for the same team and sometimes things just go a bit haywire. She seems to find the kerfuffle amusing, not stressful in any way.

She also talks faster than me, which I didn't think possible. She totally rocks my world!

She explains that the contact set up plans of a roadside meet with another OrphFund volunteer at a halfway point but that had all got lost in translation.

'I think the problem is that everyone is well past their bedtime,' she laughs. 'Plus, those forty-degree days you are getting in Melbourne can't be helping.' She wasn't wrong there!

She explained that the OrphFund volunteers had been under the pump with a big project - sourcing, delivering and packing twenty-one tonnes of donations into a shipping container to be sent at the end of the week for their projects in Sierra Leone.

As often happens with these projects running entirely by volunteer power - time, resources, and indeed clear communication can be stretched thin. With Bela unravelling the miscommunication, I learn the shipping container is currently at the property of OrphFund head honcho Steve.

'Knowing of the hectic pace that is going on at their end, it might be best to arrange to get your donations direct to the shipping container. If you guys can't do that, I'll see if I can rustle up some help. But honestly I think we are running out of time and helpers so...'

'The only thing is...' she pauses, 'the shipping container is in Castlemaine.'

She waits my response. I do a quick mental calculation that its approximately two hours' drive out of Melbourne. I give a 'what do you think look?' to my friend Kaz who is still by my side packing and she nods and smiles and in her soothing voice says, 'Oh darl, let's make it a girls' road trip, you, me, and Oli!'

I am so relieved to have her support and positivity. I feel like I am being a diva, but I think of all those who worked on sorting these pencils and all the school kids in Melbourne who had donated them, and I decided to replace the 'diva' word with 'determined' instead! 'Dramatic' could also work here!

Bela and I talk some more about OrphFund and what they do in Africa supporting vulnerable children and I begin to relax a little about the adventure we are now embarking on. I realise I have been entirely caught up in myself and not thought of the children on the other end as individuals, but more of a collective group.

She tells me stories of the wonderful children and the poverty and need in their lives before OrphFund. Little children alone in the world suffering the heart-breaking effects of war, abuse, disease, and abandonment now safe and secure within the OrphFund Family. I want to know more and pester her with questions long into the night.

Over the last ten years OrphFund has built and supported eight 'Children's Villages' (orphanages), thirteen schools, numerous farming projects, water wells, micro-businesses, community partnerships, and micro-finance projects. Everything they have achieved has happened because of the hard work of their Australian and UK team of volunteers and the generosity of their donors and sponsors - mainly friends and family of the core volunteers. Every dollar of their fundraising has gone towards supporting their projects abroad, so they are truly an example of effective grass-roots change in the world.

Bela then introduces to me some of the more than 3,500 kids that they support by name and proudly relays their successes. She talks to me about the kids' opportunities now and their inspiring determination. Her love and enthusiasm are infectious. I am hooked!

Now I have a deeper understanding into the workings of OrphFund I am so excited to be working with them on this project. I am relieved that Bela took the time, taking me under her wing to show me the 'humanitarian' world from a wider perspective than just the needs of my own charity. So, despite our rocky start of miscommunications late into the night, I am excited about our impending road trip and more importantly, getting these beautiful kids some pencils!

We load up Kaz's car in the dark at well past midnight and I feel like we are on some secret mission.

Hours later and the next day comes around very quickly as we drive to Kaz's house in inner Melbourne. She has offered to drive to Castlemaine for us. This past week I have had both hands in wrist braces due to my arthritis, so driving becomes more difficult for me in those circumstances. Poor Oli is surrounded by boxes in the back with little room to move but she seems happy enough with her iPad and cheesy-mite roll. The irony of different lives for children.

We are instructed to meet a lady on the side of the road near Kaz's house to collect a few more items intended for the container ship. We are greeted by OrphFund stalwart, Mel and her husband - such lovely, warm people. We feel good about what we are doing and so do they, and we remark on how amazing it feels for strangers to come together to be able to help these children.

We set off on our journey with the radio on and a good coffee in hand. It is a fun journey on the road and spending time with Kazzie is always something I adore.

Kazzie and I met only a few years ago when I had released my second book, 'Mendemic – Inside the Man Cave'. Around the same time Kaz had completed her film called 'DAD' and was taking it up to Parliament in Canberra to share with the politicians. It was part of a campaign that we worked on and we were passionate about being advocates for children. Over the years, we formed a gorgeous friendship. Kaz is super smart and she challenges me on my opinions, which is great. In my opinion, being surrounded by smart people is so important to furthering your own intellectual prowess. She is also one of the kindest and most caring people I know.

When we arrive, it is nearly forty degrees outside. The area where we are supposed to be is dry and dusty from the days of hot weather. This Summer has been a particularly long one and it was only January. I hate to think what February and March were going to feel like, as these can often be our hotter months. Sticking out of the landscape was a gigantic orange eyesore. The shipping container is huge. On closer inspection you can see the side of it was painted 'Helping the children Sierra Leone' and 'Shine', which we later found out was painted by famous Melbourne street artists.

We hop out of the car and realise how strong the heat is and quickly find some shade and put some sunscreen on. There is no one around, no sign of anyone. We walk down the path a little and call out but no movement or sound, except for a dog barking in the distance. It's just like the wild west! We walk over to the container and around it to see if there is a note or anything to assist us. Nothing.

We find the opening, but it appears jammed and locked. We try to shift the bar, but it is really stuck.

Now I don't know whether it was the 'pressure cooker' moment or whether I was exhausted from the night before or whether the heat was getting to me. I stomp across the dirt road like a madwoman and search till I find a massive stick, more like a log really. Huffing and puffing, I stomp back to the container ship, determined to get inside. Imagine all that work and coming all this way for nothing!

With a few almighty bangs, what do you know, something shifts, and I feel like this is my first official break-in to a container ship to do good in the world. *In my defence, your honour, I am sure that if it was in fact locked, that I, said disabled person, could not have broken in to it based on my lack of strength alone.*

Looking on, I am sure someone could have said I could have had my diva moment at last, but as I said earlier, determined seems more apt.

Inside the shipping container is packed wall-to-wall-to-roof with items for the Children's Villages in Sierra Leone, and not an inch of space spared. Furniture, clothes, tools, medical supplies, and soon to be our pencils! Even solar panels that would later be used to add power points and lights to all bedrooms, classrooms, communal areas, and kitchens. Anything and everything you could think of to make a school and children's home complete. I now see the extent of the huge effort in this project!

We unload the boxes from the car and put them inside the last remaining space. I am sure it was left there just for us because everything fit perfectly. We record a quick video and take some happy photos, so we could share them with Bela and our Facebook Page for Pencils Community. We give our pencils a quick tap on the box and as we do so I say quietly to myself, 'Make it there little pencils, you can do this for the kids,' and we close up the container and left.

All in all, this container would take three months to get to Sierra Leone. It was never going to make it there easily, what with complicated customs taxes, local bribes paid and even worse - only three miles out from its destination the container was stuck on a bend in the road. Thanks to Foday and Tolo (local partners of OrphFund in Sierra Leone) a big forklift was organised and finally the orange shipping container filled with goodies made it! Twenty-one tonnes of items had found their way to the OrphFund Children's Village in Kamakwie, Sierra Leone, Africa.

OrphFund is made up of some wonderful truly dedicated volunteers. Steve Argent is the Founder and main driver. Bela, and many other dedicated volunteers have jumped on board, attracted to the grass-roots model of effective change.

With a motto of – See, Feel, Think, Do - the support OrphFund offers for the vulnerable children they meet is all driven by a need to share advantage and opportunity with some of the world's most vulnerable orphans and children.

In 2018 their fact sheet came out and it reads like this:

ORPHFUND:
- ✔ 3,500 Kids going to School
- ✔ 350 Orphans in our Homes
- ✔ 13 Schools; 8 Children's Villages
- ✔ 100 Teachers
- ✔ 4 Farms
- ✔ 40 Care workers
- ✔ 14 Toilet Blocks
- ✔ 1,500 Chickens
- ✔ 100s Trees planted
- ✔ 7 Water wells
- ✔ 75 Tonnes of Donations
- ✔ 4 Shipping Containers sent

(Source: OrphFund, 2018)

If they aren't superheroes and Humanitarian Rockstars then I don't know who is.

Even a Humanitarian Rockstar like me has to have their idols. People they look up to, aspire to be like, someone who they see as an inspiring and person of good influence. There have been a few Humanitarian Rockstars who have crossed my path, but Bela would be one of my 'standouts'.

It's hard to do a person like Bela justice! To me she is a force of nature, so determined to do right for the OrphFund children, her love and support is as loyal as they come.

When I first started Pencils, I realised I was in completely new territory. I knew nothing about running a charity and was getting by on gut instinct. Now this I still adhere to, to this day, but I have learnt to become a little more street smart and savvy thanks to Bela.

Knowing OrphFund and Bela has also assisted me in navigating the stormy waters of knowing who to trust. Without following our donations to their final destination to the kids, it can be difficult to know that everything is as it should be. Stories of ineffective, and even fraudulent onshore and offshore charities are common - especially when it comes to children's charities. Many people are right to question how much of their donation gets to the intended recipient.

The example that OrphFund (and other charities that we support) sets, is one of effective giving - making sure that the precious resources donated (whether monetary or goods) help those in the most need. It's about trusting others and trusting your gut and doing your homework!

As they run with 100% volunteer management and zero administration costs in Australia and the UK, OrphFund offer an alternative to the often bloated and expensive-to-run bigger charities.

'Even our field trips to Africa are fully self-funded! We often laugh about how the big charities pass us by in their shiny air-conditioned SUVs while we are puttering along in the dust in a convoy on the back of the cheap (and fairly dodgy) local motorbike taxis. We wouldn't have it any other way!' Bela laughs.

I have learnt to continue to trust my gut and I believe those we meet are filled with honest and authentic motives. It has been easy to steer the ship with this kind of mind set. Gut instinct and a little bit of street cred has led me to making decisions I would have otherwise struggled with in the past.

Sometimes the realities on the field are a bit too real. And these are the things that keep you up at night.

It's Easter time 2016 and we are happy on holidays at Phillip Island. I've hidden the Easter eggs for my daughter and the setting couldn't be more idyllic.

A few weeks before, we had supplied OrphFund with packages full of pencils and pencil cases for their upcoming volunteer's trip to Uganda and Kenya.

I checked in on Bela before I left, and she was happy to report:

'We have given out the pencil cases for our Kasese kids to great excitement yesterday. Then divided the rest of the pencils booty up for our Kitholi kids (up in the jungle near the Democratic Republic of the Congo border). The rest have been sent off to our Heartspring Children's Village in Kenya. That is about four hundred happy kids! Thankyou!'

Some great pictures of those gorgeous kids getting their pencil cases followed, making my heart swell with happiness.

But, in the early hours of Easter morning, my phone starts beeping. From the other side of the world I receive a very different kind of news from Bela. There have been recent issues in the town of Kasese following the killings of fifty-plus royal guards by the Ugandan police, as well as the general civil unrest in the area after the Ugandan Elections.

It's a complicated environment to say the least, however the danger has become a little too close for comfort, as a local policeman and another man had been killed in retaliation skirmishes only one hundred metres away from the Kasese Children's Village.

Bela is on Facebook Messenger with me; they are fearful of an internet blackout and I think she needs to talk about the situation with whomever is awake at home, she knows I will always answer my phone in the middle of the night if it is her.

Bela:

As you can imagine it is crazy town here with the dramas.

We are all ok - I just wanted you to know why there has been radio silence from us for the past week. We've had sporadic internet blackouts for a few days.

The children loved their pencils btw.

But the 2 deaths happened just down the road from us today. We think we are relocating the home tomorrow. We are just trying to arrange a new house to fit 47 kids asap - no biggie!!

Cindy:

Pls don't worry about pics, pencils etc your safety and the kids are the most important xxxxxx

I'm actually stunned!! Are you in full lock down mode? Is it just you and Steve handling this? Xx

Bela:

There is 7 of us from Australia here now, plus we have an amazing team of local friends + NGO friends that we trust.

Cindy:

Then firstly let's get you and the kids to safety, can you get them all out? Xxx

Bela:

Yeah – that's the plan. It's crazy - the whole town is under curfew tonight.

Cindy:

Ok! what do you need? you know I am here anytime if you need to talk.

What happens with the curfew? Not out at night or certain times? Do you need me to contact the Australian Embassy for you?

Bela:

Ah! It's not that bad yet – don't fret!

The curfew is that the local police have 'suggested' that everyone goes to bed early tonight. It's pretty surreal how casually everyone deals with this. I suppose civil unrest has to be normalised when you experience it on the reg.

Maybe it will die down to nothing tomorrow, but right now we are getting our heads around a possible evacuation for the Kasese kids.

Muzungus* (*white people in East Africa) aren't the target, so we are ok we think.

Cindy:

You know these things can change realllllly quickly though - you need to have a contingency plan!

Bela:

Yeah - we have good friends at the local MSF clinic. They have exit strategies, are well informed & keeping us up to date & will evacuate us along with them, if it comes to that.

Bela:

Plus, everyone here is on our side to do the best by the kids. Now it's just about the logistics of scraping together the funds to get the new house if needed (which we will rent) & set a whole home for the kids up in 2-3 days.

We can always hit our credit cards.

Cindy:

What helps from me? Support? Anything else? I feel helpless here for you guys xx

OMG that's insane!! What about a GoFundMe campaign?

Bela:

Don't be worried. I probably shouldn't have mentioned anything. We don't want to make this public until we are sorted and safe - our parents/spouses/ friends will freak out! So, no GoFundMe yet.

Cindy:

I am here to help and support you and the kids xx

I am a worrier – that's what I do - but I turn it into getting things done.

How can we get you money? A loan? I guess credit cards is the fastest? Hard to get money if we can't get it out to the public.

Bela:

Haha it would be a PR nightmare! Plus, we can't really deal with all the worried friends & our supporters. We may have an internet blackout soon, so it will be chaos if everyone finds out & we can't respond.

Cindy:

Is it tomorrow you find out about the new house and the move? I don't know how to drum up momentum and money for you without letting anyone know.

Bela:

Yes tomorrow.

No hysterical friends/families back home until we have a solution - ok!

I have credit cards. We can work out paying them later if needed. This is how we roll :)

Stop fretting!

The kids will be safe. It's just hectic.

Cindy:

Just want to help – it's so different when you are on the ground.

Are you sure you are ok? xx

Bela:

We will be fine. There are hundreds of Police/Army camped in town and more arriving each day. They have these amazing tanks - it's all very dramatic! The 'rebels' are small groups of men loyal to the local King.

Hey, we are off for a midnight meeting to work out our next steps.

Sorry to stress you - please don't fret.

Cindy:

You have my number, so you know you can call anytime

Bela:

And don't say I am ever boring 😊

Cindy:

Good luck - I am here if I can help you with anything. And you are never boring!

I will expect that midnight 'bail me the Fck out now please' call from Uganda xx

Sending you all my heart and safety!

Bela:

Haha - 'Bail us + our 47 kids out please thanks' 😊

Cindy:

You know they can all come live with me xx and you too! xx

I would so do it and I have a big house too x

Let me know how you go xxxx whenever you can xxx

Bela:

Thanks for the chat - I think I needed a debrief with someone in normality. Oh dear! Not so good at small talk at the moment 😊

Cindy:

xx totally understand - keep it real sister! we can do small talk another time - just reach out when you need to, and I will keep it quiet here and if I can get some money for you all then I will xx

And just like that, somewhere in the dark and with impending internet blackout in Uganda, the OrphFund team plan for their children's safety, and here on the other side of the world, we wake to smiles, chocolate, and Easter egg hunts. As we bite down into hot cross buns, I see the innocence in my child's eyes, but my heart and my mind are torn into shreds – what violence do these precious children on the other side of the world get exposed to? It's such a juxtaposition.

I was happy to learn over the coming few days and weeks that the local unrest calmed right down, and the Kasese Children's Village was not forced to evacuate in the end.

We are often updated with news of those gorgeous kids and their successes which makes me so grateful that in a complicated world, that this time…luck was on their side.

Bela's guidance has also opened us to new networks. She is quick to share any great 'pencils' opportunities she comes across and supports us along the way.

On the morning that the Les TwentyMan Foundation building burnt to the ground in Melbourne, 2016, she got in touch with me. From there we were able to make contact and get five hundred pencil cases and back to school packs together for them to continue their work in supporting local at-risk youth in Melbourne. 'Man with a Van' came on board also and helped us move the pencil cases, text books and stationery packs across town, free of charge. It was wonderful to find out that this Melbourne business does charitable work regularly.

Also, around this time, Bela told me about a friend of hers who manages a music venue in Brunswick called Rubix, who was also running a Christmas dance party project for differently abled kids. An amazing project which brings music, dancing, creativity, and art together. We were able to put together gifts as well as art and craft supplies and a Pencils volunteer drove them across town for us. More happy kids and more new friends for Pencils Community!

Such is the trust and bond that I share with Bela that I know we would do anything to help each other. An amazing individual in her own right, I know her purpose is clear, and I know she always goes the extra mile for her kids.

In my mind she couldn't be any more of a Humanitarian Rockstar - as much as she hates me calling her that! She is the most unreal and amazing person I know and as one of the most driven and assertive people, I was instantly drawn to her strength. Behind her kind nature is a strong fighter who tirelessly advocates for the welfare of the OrphFund children.

And to this day we have never met in person. Not because we haven't wanted to but more so because we are just always far too busy getting things done. In two years look at what we have created over the phone and social media. Who tells me this can't be done? No one – because we just did it. And continue to go forward every step of the way.

Dear Cindy. Hi! Do hope these are O.K. for use. Sent with good intentions.

Best Wishes, Bill & Judy

CHAPTER 5
Michelle & Jonathan (Colour Our Story; OrphFund)

'Why don't you just stay at my place?' I ask Michelle via Facebook Messenger. Communication these days is almost always through social media to begin with.

'But we haven't met before, are you sure?' she asks with concern.

'Of course, I'd love to meet you and your partner Jonathan!'

'Come and stay with Olive and I for your ten days here and besides you are coming here anyway via Africa, so it makes complete sense.'

'Only if you are sure,' she says again and then graciously accepts. The page is filled with happy emojis and a friendship is born. Such is the power of social media connection.

Michelle and Jonathan are the type of people that most people wish they could be. They travel and live true to their morals and values. Michelle is very much connected to Mother Earth and the universe and when she and Jonathan first met, they were from very different walks of life. Michelle, a massage guru and graphic designer, must have been a powerful influence on Jonathan who in complete turnaround, ditched his high-powered executive job to take on and follow more creative pursuits, such as his love for photography.

Jonathan turned his back on the corporate life, the big assets and keeping up with 'the Joneses'. He also left his older life of bacon and eggs and embraced veganism, and became a spiritual nomad with Michelle travelling around the world moving from location to location as professional house and pet sitters. Both are living each moment to the fullest in a creative and slower-paced life, expressing gratitude in a kind and loving way, not only to themselves, but to their environment. They are my kindred spirits – salt of the earth kind of people.

Without knowing it, these would be the type of people the Pencils Community attracts as the journey went on. People who want to make a difference and still believe that a difference can actually be made. Prepared to volunteer their skills and time in order to help children receive opportunity, education, and most importantly, to give them hope.

Michelle was initially put in touch with me via 'Bela' who heads up and runs the trips to Africa each year. She is a key player in OrphFund and has been volunteering and fundraising for them for many years. She is the Mama-san of the kids in Uganda and they adore her. Bela reached out to me in the December of 2015, two months after my first Facebook post took off.

As part of the forthcoming trip in March 2016 organised by Bela from OrphFund, Michelle had been organising the making of colouring books for the children in Africa, specifically Uganda (Kasese), Kenya, and Sierra Leone. The concept is this: a school in one country draws outlines in black texta on white paper. These get made into colouring books for the kids to colour in and fill in the outline. The same is done at the Kasese schools in Uganda, and the books are then swapped so that each child gets the opportunity to learn and discover what the other child's life is like. Michelle and Jonathan were part of the contingent going over to Africa to help first-hand at the school and orphanage.

The project was called 'Colour Our Story' and still exists today with beautiful colouring books being exchanged between countries, including Australia, Africa, New Zealand, and India.

This is Michelle's belief:

Colour Our Story facilitates the creation of colouring-in books and cards, by children for children, to help support vulnerable or disadvantaged children around the world. Not only do disadvantaged children become empowered, but it inspires and enables a future generation of global citizens to start caring for and uplifting one another. They are connected through the power of story and creativity - colouring across borders. Imaginations are unleashed, stories created, and stories shared.

And in Michelle's own words:

It's funny how, looking back, I'm able to clearly connect all the dots that lead to finding my WHY.

The life I have carved out for myself has been the result of many factors and life lessons, some of which were under my control and others that were not. But, despite all the challenges, my current lifestyle and vision for the future are more authentic, beautiful, and meaningful than anything I could have ever imagined!

I grew up, for the most part, lost within my own mind. A world created through an untamed imagination and dreams that knew no limits. Perhaps it was my escape from the real world that often seemed so harsh and uncaring.

Despite growing up being told repeatedly that I'm just a dreamer I chose to remain defiantly so, and I guess that explains why, as an adult, I am still drawn to the magic held within a child's mind. Something truly powerful and unstoppable comes from imaginations and dreams united and unleashed! They give us the ability to believe, influence, inspire, and create – create hope, create change, and ultimately create a better future.

For the longest time I imagined I would one day write and illustrate children's books, but I could not have envisaged the path that lead me here. COLOUR OUR STORY aims to draw out young imaginations and facilitates a beautiful, creative exchange between children from such different parts of the world with different backgrounds and experiences. These books could help ignite a deeper sense of global community and humanity across borders and oceans, starting with the young ones and eventually reaching the older generations.

However, what had the greatest impact on me, spending creative time with kids in remote places in Asia and Africa, is that having a creative outlet and being encouraged to express themselves goes so much deeper! It led me to further research and discover the therapeutic benefits of creative activities for children who have suffered trauma and loss. From my own personal experience volunteering with children I do believe the benefits of creative expression and freedom are profound! If more children grew up with this opportunity just imagine the changed and more deeply connected global community and world we could create.

My name is Michelle Euinton, and this is my little project with a big heart and a bright, promising future.'

When Michelle arrives in Melbourne in March 2016 I am recovering from major surgery. Although sore and tired, her beautiful energy empowers me and we have many a late-night conversation about making good in the world and of course this takes place in the Pencils Boardroom (the balcony with wine or the vineyard with wine on especially hot days)! We pour out our hearts and share our stories, hopes, traumas and open up honestly to each other.

When Jonathan joins us a few days later, he immediately joins the 'new best friends brigade' and fits into the house beautifully. You know you can tell when people are magical is the way they treat your children. The love and games that they engaged in with Oli endeared them both to me in a very special way. I feel so lucky to have beautiful friends like this in our life.

The days go too fast and soon we are at the tail end of their Melbourne stay. Michelle's colouring books are printed via my connection with Ocean Reeve and the delight on her face and sparkling eyes as she opens the box and looks at them for the first time, is priceless. The local op shops get raided for old suitcases and we proceeded to pack over 80kg of stationery items in the suitcases for both Jonathan and Michelle. Once they arrived, the items would be sorted and distributed to all the children in the orphanage.

The day finally arrives, and Michelle and Jonathan are taken to the local bus stop. Over six suitcases are loaded up along with a small bag of clothes and personal items for themselves. They sacrifice space in their clothes in order to fit more pencils in. I haven't seen my friends for two years now, but nothing changes between us. We Skype and dream up ideas together and right now, Michelle has created an online auction for artwork from around the world. One day we are hoping to have a Pencils Art Gallery in which to house local artwork and sell it, with the money returning to the children and communities in which they live. But more on that later.

I will never forget the photos of the children that were sent back from this trip. It made me really understand the connection of what we were doing. On our end packing pencil cases, on the other end, children now with opportunity and a real chance at education with all the right resources. Their eyes and smiles stole my heart and I was hooked on helping them all as much as I could.

Dear Cindy. What a wonderful plan. I've included in this package a few other items you may be able to use. Best wishes to you and your project. I read about your pencil help in 'The Weekly Times'.

Margaret H.

CHAPTER 6
Schools, community, and volunteers

I remember about half way through 2016 I was in the Pencils room sorting pencils with my good friend Lise. Now Lise is one of these very spiritual people able to read you and situations very well, and I think she is a bit psychic. I ask her whether she thinks I should keep Pencils small.

'You know Lise, just keep it as a hobby. That way I don't have to apply to be an official charity or look into getting a warehouse or all those big scary things. Should I keep it small or let it grow big?'

She is sorting pencils and stops and looks at me with her warm brown eyes.

'Cin,' she says in a soft and knowing voice, 'it already is big!' and she laughs gently. She knows that the penny has not quite dropped for me yet.

She's right! Only six months since I started, this 'Mumsy' hobby of mine, and it is taking off with gusto! I think a lot about it in my spare time which is getting less and less as I am getting hungrier to make this a success. Why? So that we can help more kids.

Every time I post on Facebook and answer messages, the more Pencils Community builds. And the more it builds, the more children I can help and reach. I've received back photos by now and when you look into the happy smiles and laughing faces of children, and know you are responsible, it changes you.

Running a charity (which Pencils officially is not at this stage) is teaching me a lot about human connection. By pure luck, we also struck gold with our model. A supply chain that is regular, a gift that is in high demand in remote communities and around Australia and the world and handily, doesn't have a shelf life.

The other part of the Pencils model is that it is easy. An easy-to-understand concept for everyone. It makes people feel good that their items, their children's items, instead of ending up in landfill, are instead used as a tool for another child's education, providing both hope and opportunity.

We are lucky enough to have support from friends near and afar. People donate what they can in terms of pencils and stationery, but we were extremely lucky to receive generous offers of shelving also. My good friend, John, donated a shelf that was extremely solid. It was our one shelf that we had until the beginning of 2018! We still love that shelf dearly and it has prize positioning in the Pencils room.

The moving train, keeps moving and I am now beginning to be invited to schools. In 2016 we will visit over fifty schools and discuss Pencils and the issues that children face around the world. In 2017 we will visit one hundred and fifty schools. People want to see the face behind the name and the kids love getting the chance to ask questions. We have had our logo updated by a professional graphic designer and we have started to embody a more professional approach. The more seriously we are taken, the better our chances to get in front of the right people.

For me, talking at schools is also a way to get out and about in my community and keep engaged and keep my finger on the pulse about what the schools need from us. Doing talks and workshops at schools is a way for me to give back to the community and helps to foster the junior leaders of tomorrow.

In many schools, they have social justice committees whose role is to look for worthwhile activities and ways in which young school students can make a difference. By uniting Pencils and the school community, we've been able to create a synergy and an avenue to demonstrate real change to students. They can see the pencil cases that they donate being held up months later by a child in Asia who previously did not own one. We feel then that the concept goes full circle for a student, to embrace a thought, followed by an action, to a result, and know that they are responsible.

The power of that is immense.

The students have been taught to critically evaluate the charity sector and ask the tough questions. I loved it the first time a nine-year-old asked me why 90 cents in the dollar doesn't get to the child at the end. They love it when we can answer them with authenticity about why our charity is 100% volunteer run and operates out of the bottom of my house.

Whenever we are out talking about Pencils in schools or at other presentations we always discuss our big three, education, sustainability, and humanitarian issues.

Education is our big one as it works two-fold. We not only get to provide educational items for our children in need, but we get to educate our own children about issues that face the wider world, social issues. It also gives us an opportunity to discuss gratefulness and mindfulness. We often have a child on the Autism spectrum or one suffering from anxiety able to get up in front of their class and talk about the importance of collecting pencils – a huge achievement.

I remember one little girl was so nervous to present she threw up in the toilets before her presentation. Whether the whizzy dizzies at lunch time or the nerves, she still got up in front of seven hundred children and parents and spoke of pencils and how she took them on a family holiday to Bali and what it meant to her seeing the children, from her eyes. Now I don't know many adults that would publicly speak in front of seven hundred people. She got through her presentation like a star and she still is my special little champion.

We are also being incredibly supported by the same schools each year. Small, public government schools would become our biggest supporters and donators of pencils and stationery. Schools such as, GlenHuntly Primary School, supported us regularly with donations. My gorgeous friend, Ruthie, a teacher at the school has been a huge supporter of us from the beginning, as have many other primary schools in the Brighton and Bayside areas thanks to our relationships with the teaching staff.

Many schools were surprised to learn that children in remote parts of Australia were as severely impacted by lack of educational items as the kids were in Africa and elsewhere in the world. Even some school children in Melbourne city were unable to afford a pencil case.

In our two-year history we have supplied over 1,000 pencil cases and back-to-school packs to various organisations like the Les Twentyman Foundation and Prahran Mission for the kids of Melbourne. I still find that one of the hardest situations to fully grasp, that in Melbourne, my beautiful city, that the poverty level could be so extreme. Having travelled the world for many years you always think with rose coloured glasses that surely the politicians and councillors here would never let it be that extreme, but it is. Open eyes and open minds are needed here and everywhere.

In classrooms across Melbourne, we create specific projects for the kids. We run different collection campaigns, have 'dress up as your favourite colour' day, create a colouring book, and sponsor a box. This is where the children fundraise, but the money goes directly to the project (so they buy a box and pay for the shipping of that box to their destination of choice). This works extremely well if the school is studying a particular country or culture and can therefore send their box to a school in Cambodia, Fiji, or remote communities in Australia.

Sustainability is also increasing in interest and although it is not the most exciting of topics, Australia now creeps into fifth place as one of the largest waste producers in the world. This is a statistic that we should not be proud of. We have big ideas in 2018 to start implementing more recycling options as we strategize and find ways to improve at Pencils HQs.

And the consequence of being engaged with the community like this can have some surprising results.

I had been invited on a trip to Mt Isa with my friend Ocean to help him present his famous Publishing Seminar. Ocean is Australasia's #1 Author Success Coach. He helps facilitate the creative process for those willing to write a book and is an award-winning publisher, author, and international speaker in his own right.

Between catching planes in Brisbane to 'the Isa' I receive a call:

'Hi, is that Cindy from Pencils?' the female voice asks me.

At this point I'm holding the phone against my ear with a sore shoulder as I try and juggle hand-luggage and my boarding pass. The flights to Mt Isa are small planes and the queue moves quickly.

'Yes, it is' I say, 'How can I help?'

'Our company is going paperless and I wondered if you want some stationery supplies? We would pay for it to be delivered to you. It's six floors' worth.'

The airhostess is looking at me with a 'Get off your phone' expression.

'I beg your pardon; did you say six floors?'

I cannot ignore the airhostess any longer and Ocean and I are hurried through the gates to board the plane. In twenty metres I must turn off my phone, so I can walk onto the tarmac and board the small aircraft. I quickly agree to the delivery and give them my address.

This was quite possibly the least thought-through decision of Pencils I've ever made, but it turned out to be a blessing.

It is late in the evening when I arrive back home from my trip. My mum looked after Olive while I was away, and when she opens the door I just about faint. The downstairs room is full of boxes all the way to the roof! Being late I say a quick hello with Mum and walk her out to her car and say goodbye thanking her for all her help and support. She makes it possible for me to do trips like this.

I come back inside intending to throw my clothes straight into the washing machine, as you do when you first come back from a trip. Olive is fast asleep, and I remember last minute, that there was a dirty tea-towel in the back room from before I had left for the trip. So, I decided to go grab it.

The first I knew that the washing machine had flooded, was when I slipped in the cold water. I slammed down hard on the concrete floor, using my wrist and forearm to break my fall. After a decade of cortisone treatments, I don't have strong wrists at the best of times. I lay there in agony trying not to vomit from the pain, knowing for sure I have broken something. After ten minutes of crying in pain, and lying in a wet puddle on the concrete floor in the dark, I thought, who's going to help me now? It was excruciating but I managed to work my way out of my t-shirt and use it as an impromptu bandage. I wrapped it as tight as I could around my forearm tightening it with my teeth. I got to my knees and shakily stood up, the whole time cradling my wrist.

After climbing the eternity of stairs, I grabbed some painkillers and spent the rest of the night sitting on the couch with a blanket in agony, questioning whether half a bottle of wine would help at all, and whether it was worth moving to get it. The upshot of my accident? I did, indeed, fracture my wrist.

I decided that there was no way that I could even open a box, let alone lift one, so I posted a request on my Facebook Page. A few days later thirty people showed up. By magic, wine and barbeque appeared, and somehow by the end of the day, all the boxes were organised and categorised.

This became the first official Pencils Community sorting day, because strangers just turned up to help. I was so grateful, and they were so kind. All the prior sorting days before were close friends and family, yet now I realised that strangers with a common cause wanted to help. And this was a great way to get things done. And all it took was an immense amount of stationery and a damaged wrist to make me realise it. I guess I should add stubborn to determined.

We now regularly have Pencils Community sorting days and the kids come along to help. As one mum said to us, 'You are the only charity that we know of where the children can come and help and be involved.'

Many people find it hard to ask for help from others; I know I do. Yet my experience with Pencils tells me that most people want to help, but they just don't know how.

They have busy lives, careers, and families, so their time is often limited. However, finding them ways in which they can help in Pencils has been relatively easy because we are flexible. We have some people who take a box of mix match pencils and sort them over the school holidays with their kids, teaching them the value of charity work along the way.

Without community involvement, Pencils Community would not run as productively as it does. But not only do we meet the practical elements of sorting and repurposing pencils and stationery, we have a lot of fun on our community days. Being united in a purpose brings us all closer together. Every person brings with them a unique skill set.

There are many volunteers who've joined Pencils from the beginning and through to now. Such as, Monique, Jules, Jess, Val, Gaynor, Ange, Gail, Lise, Charmaine, Lynne, Yvonne, Phyllis, Sheena, and of course

Mum and Oli. They all have a great laugh, they come when they can and pack pencils and help with projects and when other life events and work cross over, they take a break and return when they like. As 100% volunteer based, flexibility is the key.

Of course, we may have a specific project we want to complete, but with the spirit of many people coming together, things always get done. And part of the appeal, is not just helping others, but it can also be **fun**.

A Pencils sorting day usually happens like this:

I'll put a message out on Facebook for a sorting day a few weeks beforehand. Regulars turn up, and usually one or two newbies, who have heard about us through the power of social media. If I bribe them with food and wine, people come in droves. I think that it's because they want to help, but the hospitality is appreciated and doesn't go unnoticed.

We all settle into a 'job' that we like, whether it be sorting, sharpening, or bundling the pencils into a bunch of ten to twelve, one of each colour.

After a while things get a bit silly and the laughter starts. When you are trying to sort colours and find a two-tone pencil (red on one end, and blue on the other) they totally screw with your mind, and laughter usually follows.

'What happens in the Pencils room stays in the Pencils room,' is our long-standing principle. Whether it be the cathartic nature of sorting or the monotonous nature of it, it seems to allow people the opportunity to talk about their lives, their feelings, or their relationships. We have many a friend who has opened up to reveal something important going on in their life and you can see that they feel better by openly talking about it with others.

Often, I would think to myself after a particularly big revelation, that Pencils isn't actually about pencils at all. It's about connection to one another and community.

One of these sticks in my mind because it made me realise the cathartic nature of doing something as simple as sorting pencils. Previously I'd found it helpful to me. Sorting pencils is a good workout for my hands, but I had never fully realised it could provide not just physical therapy. I got a thank you from a parent, who in the midst of their grief at the death of their partner, sorted pencils for hours with their young child. For those hours they bonded together in a shared task when everything around them felt like too much to handle. Such a simple thing as sorting pencils, yet so powerful.

Olive (Oli), my daughter, now nine years old, and her little friends, Georgia, Trin, Aaliyah, John Junior, and Ruby take coffee and lunch orders on the pencils days. They have seen to their role as being the hostesses of the day, and this is intermingled with finding the 'coolest' Smiggle items for the other kids overseas and testing textas. Mostly it's about socialising for them, but they are starting to understand more.

One night we are watching the movie Lion, a movie about an Indian boy who gets lost on the railways in India and then is ultimately adopted out to an Australian family. As an adult, he always had a burning question as to where he was from. He then manages to find his way back to a little town in India through the study of Google Maps, retracing his steps and memory as a child. It's a true story and you see plenty of scenes about the level of poverty in India.

Oli turns to me in the middle of the movie with big wide eyes and says, 'Ohhhhh… so that's why we do Pencils, I get it now!' It's a beautiful moment for me as her Mum to see her grasp the greater world around her. I am grateful for the path that life has taken me on and that this is something I can show her and that she can develop as she gets older.

As the journey of pencils continues, towards the end of 2017, we attempted our first textbook recycle program with great success. Old textbooks made their way to our headquarters, but as we are limited on space we had to limit it to one car load per school. Over the Summer we move twelve tonnes of text books into a ute tray truck with our friends from St Vinnies who then took them on to be recycled.

In 2018, we will streamline this method more, contemplating a big giant skip in my driveway for the month of December; the neighbours will be so pleased! Actually, they are unreal and will come and help so I am lucky to be where I am.

We will also look at a pilot program to be trialled in a Melbourne school, already run successfully in Queensland, whereby they are able to recycle broken pens and textas that don't work anymore. Unfortunately, it always leaves me with the moral dilemma of pens and textas in other countries. Pencils are sustainable and would biodegrade essentially well, but pens and textas are covered in a plastic coating so I am left with the decision of should we send or not send? What are the waste minimisation practices in these countries? Do they even exist? Are we just increasing landfill and our carbon footprint or are we providing something greater? Is it a tool for change that may one day solve these problems?

I hope it's the latter, but in my lifetime, I will probably never know. I do however have to believe that it will make the difference in the end and so I push on with it. There are always two ways to look at every situation.

By the end of 2017 we have grown so big that my gorgeous volunteer Val steps up and helps organise the warehouse. A declutter specialist, she works hard and tirelessly and gets the warehouse into shape with clear plastic tubs, so we can see all our items and colours clearly. We get a 3m x 3m shed built in the front driveway to act as a holding pen as we anticipate a lot of December deliveries. Val has now become my 2nd In Command and I couldn't be more thrilled.

One day she picks me up in the car and says, 'Let's go to Bunnings and ask about shelving.' And in true Pencils style, we walk in and she greets an old friend who works there. He in turn sends us straight to speak with Rob, the main community activity coordinator. Just like that, in a sweet fifteen minutes, the promise of shelving has occurred. One letter stating who we are, and the wheels are in motion.

Everything that happens with Pencils happens organically. We don't go out and push, we let the universe come to us with what it's meant to. Were we meant to walk in that day and get free shelves in fifteen minutes or were we meant to fight hard for this?

There are so many examples of this sort of thing for Pencils. We have the banks ringing us, we have Big W and Officeworks help where they can. However, the main drivers of all of this comes from the mums and dads and the kids who believe that this is a great cause and a simple one to support. Everyone just needs to find their special groove and make their mark; it's about what makes them happiest and that's how we run smoothly and efficiently.

To Cindy, I read your story in 'The Weekly Times' as I have been sorting through my wife's things, since she passed away back in 2009. She was a happy Primary School Teacher, all her working life, as you can see has collected a few pencils and books. So, I thought I would send them on to you. Could come across more at another time.

Claude R.

CHAPTER 7

The Global Community Come on Board as Real People

Cultivating relationships and connecting people seems to be my strongest skillset. Yet remember this book is about the amazing journey of the last couple of years. It is about celebrating the kind of people I've met along the way. The 'humanitarian rockstars'. You might have a journey and destination in mind, but the people that you meet along the way are what make the journey more than time and distance, but an experience you'll remember forever.

What began as a few emails and Facebook messages, after three years has become one to two hundred per week. Although I have a background in communications, every email or message is about connecting with each individual authentically. As I often say, it hurts just to talk some days, so why would I waste my time being anything but true to myself and my passion? There is no trying to 'cajole' or win anyone over, it's about pure truth and common goals.

By being this way and representing Pencils, it has resulted in attracting similar people. Like attracts like, so it has been my pleasure to meet and befriend the most amazing individuals on my journey.

People have touched my heart through Pencils, and I am extremely grateful to them. I feel that my volunteers, each and every one of them, are Humanitarian Rockstars, as are all the children who are recipients of Pencils, and all the children who are our suppliers of pencils and who gain understanding everyday of what it means to be a humanitarian. New and beautiful spirited volunteers arrive daily from the likes of Jo, Connie, Mariela, and of course our core group keeps coming back for more and more – how lucky are we!

We also attract organisations to us who come on board to help. We have worked with Scouts, Church groups, Commonwealth Bank, Lions Clubs, Rotary, OrphFund, SANCSS, Footys4All, Ceres, Ocean Reeve Publishing, and so many more that it would be another whole book in itself.

So here are some very special friends of Pencils that we have worked with in helping kids in Australia and around the globe. I want to now give you a little taste of the wonderful people and world in which we live, which I think will surprise you. We have worked with them all and hold them in the highest regard. They are our tribe and village whom we protect and support.

You are going to read these wonderful stories in their own words:

- Jaime Ramos – SANCSS our dear friend and our most regular visitor to Pencils HQs
- Karla Eyre – Friends of Brilliant Star (Solomon Islands) My kindred Spirit
- Michael Gallus – Footys4All – All-round living legend
- Tiffany Pham – Loc Tho Orphanage (Vietnam) An amazing and strong woman who I admire immensely.

As you read through their personal stories you should see and appreciate the depth and level of human service and sacrifice that these individuals all possess. They are all so humble in this space of being humanitarians, but I take this is an opportunity and platform for them to share their personal story with you all.

You will see and understand the very definition of Humanitarian Rockstars. These individuals and associated organisations are the backbone of Pencils and people that we attract.

Why?

Because we all come together with the same purpose, just in different ways. All of us are about changing people's lives for the better, helping children, improving their quality of life and living and giving them hope and opportunities along the way that they would otherwise miss out on.

I heard about you on Lyndy Burn's radio show and thought it was a wonderful project. My son isn't at school yet so no leftover pencils. So, I bought some pencils which I bought for him which I've found are really strong.

Take Care,
Merryn H.

CHAPTER 8
Jaime Ramos - SANCSS

My Blood Runs Welfare

From the age of nineteen, I had always wanted to do something for disadvantaged kids. To set up some kind of 'home' for them and to give them a safe and secure place - a place in which to grow, have pride in themselves, and have an opportunity to thrive. For a long time, this goal was put on the backburner and appeared to be more of a pipe dream.

When just four years old, my mother, my two older sisters, my older brother, and I, the baby of the family, fled war-torn Mozambique in East Africa into neighbouring South Africa as war refugees. My father stayed behind in Mozambique for reasons that became clearer as I became an adult and so for the next fourteen years of my life, South Africa would become my home with mum and my siblings until I reached the age of seventeen years, where I would move to Western Australia.

When we first arrived in South Africa all those years ago, it was important that life had to return to normal as quickly as possible. My mum went to work each day and my sisters and brother went to school. As a four-year-old I would walk alone down the road to my Grandmother's house, which was 1.5km away – I did not speak a word of English and clearly at four years old, I learnt to become tough, resilient, and independent; this early trauma would be part of many experiences that led to my current humanitarian path. Although life had not got off to an easy start, I look back now and realise that it made me who I am today.

So, at nineteen years of age and based in Perth, I went on to study secondary teaching at Edith Cowan University and then went on to complete a Social Work Degree, all the while my focus being on disadvantaged children, specifically high-risk adolescents. My childhood experiences and now my additional twenty years of industry experience has lead me to where I find myself today - Founder of the charity SANCSS Australia Ltd that supports disadvantaged children.

SANCSS has provided support to children in need in the local community, remote Indigenous communities in Australia, children in New Zealand as well as providing support and advocacy to a Boys and Girls Home in the Philippines.

How did SANCSS come to be, and the realisation that I could now help disadvantaged children on a bigger level?

Five years ago, on November 8th, 2013, Typhoon Yolanda destroyed parts of the Philippines. 'Super Typhoon Haiyan' cut a devastating path across the central Philippines. More than 16 million people were affected across the Visayas region, where the storm is known as Yolanda.

It had a storm strength equivalent of Category Five – the highest and the strongest tropical cyclone to ever make landfall. With wind gusts up to 375 kilometres per hour and a storm surge at sea level of four metres, its impact was far reaching. I had already booked a holiday to the Philippines when the typhoon struck. The death toll was extreme – some six thousand people were killed and thousands more injured. Its impact was beyond belief.

Part of my trip was booked for Cebu and being so close to the devastated area, I couldn't holiday and go sight-seeing in the region – human nature just doesn't work like that. And, if you are someone like me, welfare is just in my blood. I had to do something.

I managed to get in touch back home with the LDS Charities (Church of Jesus Christ Latter Day Saints, or commonly referred to as Mormons), who were coordinating relief and humanitarian efforts. The LDS arranged to immediately send food and hygiene kits to church members in the affected areas and also to non-members.

With more than sixteen million people affected and with the desperate needs of people for food and shelter, Typhoon Yolanda had a massive impact on the Philippines. Allotting over $1.4 million for basic needs, the LDS set about working with the local government and other organisations in the assessment of the situation and the distribution of relief goods.

After arriving in Cebu and organising my relief effort with LDS Charities, I left on a boat from Cebu to Ormoc. I got off the pier and there was a stranger holding a sign with my name on it. It felt very surreal, the devastation visible from the pier was something I had never experienced before.

Once there, I travelled around and checked in on local building projects and temporary accommodation relief projects. With my experience and training in trauma and trauma recovery I was able to really help on the ground. I stayed in a tiny hotel that I shared with some cockroaches. I asked if I could be taken to some local orphanages to see how they were going.

Two of the centres I visited were the Boys' and Girls' Home/Centres in Ormoc. The Boys' Centre was in total disrepair. The more I learnt of this place the more it got in under my skin. There were broken windows, holes in the roof, and the boys were treated like animals. They were a combination of street kids, petty criminals, and sometimes children who had committed serious offences – all grouped together. Can you imagine an orphaned street kid in the same room as a criminal? But here they were, treated like animals, locked up at night and in their lunch break so they would not run away. The kids were between the ages of six and eighteen and seemed more like prisoners than an orphanage or home.

The Boy's home also had two male adults who were intellectually disabled living in the home and it was the job of the six-year-old to wipe their bums. It broke my heart and the first thing I wanted to do was give the boys some dignity back along with fixing some of the basic repairs, like painting, showers, and food.

The Boys' Home ranged from about fifteen to thirty kids at any one time. The Girls' Home consisted of girls that were more stable in terms of their comings and goings, with approximately twenty-two girls present.

The World Health Organisation put this disaster (Typhoon Yolanda) on par with the 2004 Indian Ocean tsunami and the Haiti earthquake in 2010. The most immediate threat to survivors was the lack of safe drinking water, no shelter, untreated injuries and illness, insufficient food, lack of sanitation and personal hygiene items, and lack of household supplies like fuel. Ironically, this is what the Boys' and Girls' Homes faced almost daily and not from a horrific natural disaster.

When I returned home to Australia, I knew something had changed. I no longer spent my money on materialistic items, instead saving money to personally send, source items, or go back to the Boys' and Girls' Home to assist in Ormoc. Since Typhoon Yolanda, the need for services to care for disadvantaged children had risen with government services being unable to cope.

Many of the government experiences we faced with the Boys' Home showed up the cultural differences and bureaucratic nightmares we faced. Red tape was an understatement, as were the levels of the corruption. What that meant directly on the ground, was that these children did not even have their basic needs met. My blood was pumping, so I decided to change things…for the better.

I got together with a group of friends and professionals who were also passionate about the care and wellbeing of the children and set up the Not-For-Profit / Charity called SANCSS Australia Ltd 'SANCSS' – which stands for Sanctuary Services.

SANCSS Australia Ltd was established to help children in Australia, New Zealand, the Philippines as well as other countries overcome barriers to life including accommodation, education, health, drugs, alcohol, and more. Part of the initial aim being to achieve the establishment of residential care homes and the implementation of programs to help educate youth and their families that are affected by this in specific regions of the Philippines.

The vision and goal of the organisation is to be a leading provider of care and support for disadvantaged children. Everyone who is a part of SANCSS is dedicated to providing assistance to disadvantaged children.

I could now use my knowledge and experience in the government and non-government welfare sector to know exactly what and how I wanted my charity to be like. I didn't want to go 'corporate' or have money donated that went on admin. I wanted every cent and every volunteer's help and time, as well as my own, to go directly to the kids. As long as, the kids are 0-18 years old, then I am happy to help them. We have no discrimination towards our children – we only want to help.

Through SANCSS we have been able to achieve so much in our two and a half years since forming. We have improved the Boys' and Girls' Centres' living conditions, repaired, replaced, and painted so that it could feel more like a home. We have fixed holes in the roof so that they can still cook meals even when it's raining. A rainwater harvesting project provides running water to a small school, saving the children a long walk with buckets to collect water.

Each and every trip to the Philippines, has been paid for personally by the volunteers.

We also organised dental projects so that the kids could eat properly and smile, which is what you want when you give them their dignity back. We have been able to keep the kids in school and help other local schools in the district and have helped source books for school libraries. We are working with the local government and education department in Omroc to set up and operate a resource centre that contains groups of items that the children / schools can borrow – resources like sporting equipment, encyclopaedias, art and craft, and more. And yes, we put an end to six-year-olds caring for disabled adults.

We work closely with Pencils Community and other organisations that help supply these pencils and stationery items – even sourcing two microscopes for a big school in the city of Ormoc, the kind that you would see at any standard secondary school in Australia. We have been able to achieve so much to improve the lives of the children, creating hope and a future for them. I regularly come to Pencils HQs and load up my jeep full of goodies and have been able to source other wonderful items such as laptops and numerous items from community members and other companies.

Poverty will always be a part of life in the Philippines. But that doesn't mean we should ever give up on caring and trying. These kids were once treated like animals. We have advocated to give them back their respect and pride on many levels, from adequate living, hygiene and nutrition to schooling. We meet regularly now with the local Mayor of Ormoc and officials to get things done at the Boys' and Girls' Centre. Our goal is to keep reaching and moving forward to improve their lives and see what can happen.

In Australia and New Zealand, we continue to support our local and indigenous kids as well. We have shipped boxes and pallets filled with educational items to those in need and helped many disadvantaged children. We continue to accompany all our items to their destination ensuring they get there safely, or we make sure we have a connection with someone there that we know is legit and authentic. People feel confident supporting a charity like ours knowing this.

Just in the last year alone, we know that forty different schools donated items to SANCSS which found their way to the Philippines, New Zealand and Australian children and as a result we have helped approximately 5,000 children in the last financial year.

We have many new projects and initiatives to get off the ground and we will continue to move SANCSS forward in a way in which it stays truly authentic and not corporate and is always, all about helping the children.

I guess we all have gaps in our life that we try to fill. Some people fill them with alcohol, gambling, addictions, or other. I fill my life with helping disadvantaged children. My passion to help runs through my veins and is in my DNA. Whether that is attributed to my childhood experiences or not, I suspect it is. I grew up without a father and was twenty-seven when he died. I guess as the baby of the family and then a boy growing up without my Dad that this was a key part to my development and wish to help other young boys who might be in a similar situation, experiencing similar emotions.

To say that welfare runs through my veins would be an accurate way to measure the man that I am today. I am forty-seven years old and am the Founder and chairman of SANCSS Australia Ltd; more importantly, I give disadvantaged kids a start in life that they would otherwise miss out on.

Dear Cindy. What a delightful surprise to receive your lovely letter. It is amazing that, for such a busy and achieving person you took time to write to me, so THANK YOU. Writing is a 'thing' that those of us who can, take for granted. As for a letter/note/card – they are almost obsolete, but not so for some of us, thank goodness. Thank you again for your letter and kind words,

Judy W.

CHAPTER 9

Karla Eyre - Friends of Brilliant Star (Solomon Islands)

My Journey with Brilliant Star.

With a background in early childhood education, a marriage breakdown, and total mind, body and spiritual collapse which triggered three types of arthritis in my body, I knew it was time to change my life. I had been a workaholic, but it never filled the desire in me to serve humanity on the level I wanted. I had done some smaller projects with a school in Tonga, but it had just ended. It was a bittersweet experience, as the teachers had become independent. I felt redundant! The very next day I was asked by a friend if I could help Brilliant Star, an extremely poor school in the Solomon Islands. The answer was yes, even though I had no idea what I was about to embark on.

I did have the feeling this was huge, so I decided to form a board of directors, a great group of people with different skills, who just seemed to fall into place and then take the journey of writing a constitution and registering. This was in 2017. We are a very tiny charity, but everything goes to the school and the children. We have no office, and we all pay our own way to Solomon's. We meet on Skype. It was important to me that money goes to what people donate it for. We only have accountancy fees.

I first visited the school in October 2017. To be greeted at the airport by the children holding banners and placing leis over my head, I was overwhelmed and hugged every child. Next day I arrived at the school. On the physical level a collection of hut buildings, next to no water, two toilets for 200 children, no doors, no lockable class-rooms, no resources, untrained, and unpaid teachers. I had arrived at Brilliant Star.

The children were amazing, happy to be at school and bubbling over. The teachers were dedicated, humble, and resilient and my heart was taken. I realised nothing I would go through would be harder than the daily dedication of these amazing souls to educate the children in that region. Solomon Islands has hundreds of children with no education and now it was to be part of my journey and I thanked God for the blessing.

I had carried a bag of art supplies thinking they would be for kindy. How wrong could I be? The school were preparing for the bicentenary of two hundred years of the birth of Baha'u'llah and I was asked if all the students could please use some materials to make an invitation for their family. I had to stop children and promise they could come the next day and they all eagerly wanted to be in the class. Of course, the little ones love the art but again I was so taken when I watched the older boys aged about fifteen or so gently separate colours and so thoughtfully create their card.

They took hours … I explained to the principal that I was amazed in the way they used the materials, only to be told they had never used any paints or collage before. Another humbling moment. We do simple things that we take for granted here and then find how huge the impact is over there. From that time on, I have been dedicated to these students being able to have materials to create. Imagine a society with no oppor-tunity to learn and create.

We had set up Facebook and Go Fund Me and very slowly donations came in. We managed to buy a generator in the first year. It arrived when I was at the school - the excitement and joy of having some electricity. They talked of being able to have events, eventually have educational videos, run a photocopier, build new desks, improve buildings. They used the generator at their big event and were able to have lights at night and ran an outdoor movie for the children who slept at the school all night.

I came back and worked harder to get funds with a focus on the literacy of the children as there was no set program and the levels right through the whole country are low. I have been so blessed to have generous souls come into my life who are donating essential materials.

Emma Lewis is helping with literacy. It is expensive to get things there but as I write this I am in awe. A ship is on the way with pencils and stationery from beautiful Cindy, as well as early childhood materials for the kindy and prep that I purchased.

This is life-changing for this school. Every step takes them to higher levels of education. Spataps came and delivered their wonderful device, so now children can wash their hands. These things seem so basic, but they are life-changing. The lack of hygiene causes viruses and bugs in children, so they can't attend school.

It is 2018 I don't know why there is so much imbalance in the world. Every child should have an education as a right to a better life and future to help their community. I'm heading back in four weeks, so excited, so many new things starting to happen. I have written the curriculum for kindy and prep and am training teachers there. I have suitcases full of literacy materials going with me, but I know no matter what I think I'm doing, I will be shown something new.

I feel humbled to be involved with Brilliant Star. They are a shining light in Solomon Islands. A proof that others do care about them even though they are remote, even though they have few resources, but they are resilient and strong and because of good people we will bring more children the joy of education. I am blessed.

Pencils Community for me is a 'DREAM COME TRUE'.

Five years ago, I gave a talk in Hawaii about my ultimate dream to help Indigenous children, however I had no idea as to how and when that would happen, but I remained optimistic and retained an awareness for opportunities and it has come through Pencils Community, I'm so excited.

The reality of being able to physically volunteer in a humanitarian organisation that helps children is such a wonderful feeling for me and the laughter and sharing by volunteers while sorting the pencils that have been donated, is an extra joy.

THANK YOU, Founder/CEO of Pencils Community.

Phyllis O'Connor

CHAPTER 10

Michael Gallus (Footys4All)

Changing Kids' Lives One Ball at A Time.

Six years nearly to the day, Footys4All volunteer founding director Michael Gallus was inspired by the words of South African World Leader Nelson Mandela, who stated that, *'Sport speaks to youth in a language that they understand. It is more powerful than governments, race, and religion in creating hope where there once was despair. It has the power to inspire. It has the power to unite people in a way that little else does.'*

Thanks to this quote I had my own dream to provide hope and a sporting opportunity through the gift of a new ball to children in need across Australia and around the world.

I had just turned forty years of age and went into the usual midlife crisis mode with the stark realisation that I was more likely to die during the next forty years than I had been in the first forty years. Flawed logic, but that was my thoughts. Most men I hear from during their midlife crises trade their wives in for the younger, usually blonde, girlfriend and buy a red sports car. I did something even more crazier for my midlife crisis I started my own charity.

As a teacher at Penleigh and Essendon Grammar school for sixteen years, junior community and AGSV (The Associated Grammar Schools of Victoria) sporting basketball, cricket, and football coach, father of three children, AFL (Australian Football League) TV and radio commentator, Brisbane Lions Victorian based part time AFL recruiter, I had seen how the power of sport could produce a positive pathway for youth in so many ways.

Over all those years, I had seen how sport teaches participants of both genders, many cultures, races, and religions about team work, courage, resilience, dedication, determination, concentration, defeat, humility, and victory in an environment that also improved the participants physical and mental state of mind.

With childhood obesity and disease rates such as juvenile diabetes on the rise, combined with many youth embarking on a negative life pathway of drugs, alcohol, and crime due to heartache, boredom, and being easily misled, I had seen first-hand, how that the power of sport, as Nelson Mandela stated, 'spoke to youth in a language that they understood.'

My midlife crisis was in full swing and as Aberfeldie Auskick coordinator, I had been given $3,000 to upgrade the centre's equipment, thanks to a generous donation by a local business man Michael Egan. Michael had asked if a third of the donation could be used in some way to benefit disadvantaged children in sport. I answered of course and went and purchased a variety of sporting balls, which I sent to friends, to distribute to children, who were teaching in remote Aboriginal communities.

I dropped some balls off myself to the children in the Sunshine and Maldon women's prisons and Broadmeadows detention centre. I received photos of smiling children, letters of thanks and glowing stories of the impact that had been made all through the simple gift of a new ball.

This got me thinking of how I could replicate this act of gaining donations, purchasing balls and then distributing them to children in need on a local, state, national, and international scale. I thought that all I had to do was link up all the kind, caring, and empathetic people I had met throughout my teaching, media and community coaching careers and we could as an inspirational Indian world leader stated, 'Be the change we wanted to see in the world.'

I came up with the name Footys4All then spoke with the most beautiful, patient, caring and understanding wife in the whole world who agreed that she would support me, and the journey had begun.

My life as a husband, father, son, brother, teacher, and coach continued on in addition to setting up the Footys4All charity. Something had to give as my hours of sleep rapidly diminished and my energy levels decreased. To continue on with this maniacal lifestyle which I had dedicated myself to, I changed my life.

I gave up alcohol, which was one of the best decisions of my life both financially and physically. I had taken binge drinking to a new level, seeing me hospitalised three times. It got to the point that the aftermath of a big night saw me scaring my children as I struggled physically to cope with the devastating negative effects of alcohol.

It took another three years before I could admit that I was an alcoholic in the form of a binge drinker and realise that drinking alcohol for me had to stop, period. I am now very proud to say I have not had any alcohol for three years and don't miss it one bit. I also stopped drinking coffee, looked at what I was eating, and changed my diet to a healthier regime of fruits and vegetables and exercised more consistently. These changes enabled me to work the sixteen to twenty hours a day that I needed to get everything done.

There was so much to do to set up Footys4All, that at times it was overwhelming. Yet the impact of the photographs of the smiling children, and the joyful anecdotes I had received from the Michael Egan donation, kept burning into my brain. I knew if I didn't continue that these children around Melbourne, Victoria, Australia, and the world would miss out on what the rest of us took for granted.

I ploughed on and there is no other way to describe it. One foot in front of the other. One meeting after another after work, before work, during school holidays, late at night, and early in the morning, squeezed in wherever I could, and Footys4All began to take shape due to amazing support.

Setting up a successful volunteer charity such as Footys4All only happened due to the inspiring and amazing support from all that I met with and spoke to. Every single man, woman and child asked, 'how can I help?' which in turn inspired me to work harder and longer to get this charity up and running.

I cannot thank enough my wife Amanda, children Thomas, Lily and Benjamin along with my parents Geoff and Lois Gallus, and father-in-law and mother-in-law Kim and Irene Packer, along with every supporter, volunteer and sponsor, for getting on board with Footys4All to change kids' lives one ball at a time. The Footys4All family community had been created.

I won't bore you with all the details of all the bloody hard work, tears, struggles, laughter, triumphs, tribulations, victories, and defeats over the last six years and boy had there been a few. Suffice to say it has been a marathon, not the sprint I thought it would be when I first thought of the idea of creating this charity. But today here we stand proudly with over twenty-two thousand new balls of hope and new sporting opportunity delivered across Victoria, around Australia, and out to the world. We've reached kids in such close and far flung places as Africa, India, Fiji, New Zealand, Nepal, Thailand, and Vietnam.

Community recognition flows in furthering inspiring the Footys4All family that we were on the right track with awards such as the Spirit of the City of Moonee Valley, Pride of Australia Medal and just recently Footys4All was honoured and humbled as one of sixty Victorian volunteers out of the 1.5 million in the state to receive the Premier of Victoria's champion volunteer Impact Award at an overwhelming ceremony at government house.

The present and future work continues, as we speak to State and Federal governments as well as corporate businesses for funding, with a goal to distribute balls to thirty thousand very special needs and underprivileged children via one hundred and twenty schools in Victoria. We continue to support and engage with remote Aboriginal communities and I take the time here to thank the Aboriginal people of Melbourne and Australia for allowing us into their communities, schools, sporting clubs and hearts to show that Footys4All truly does believe in reconciliation and respect for the traditional custodians of this great land.

The Footys4All family has learnt so much about Aboriginal music, art, language, food, culture, and most importantly about the importance of family from all of our engagements with Aboriginal people. We are truly honoured and thankful for the experience and the more time I spend with Aboriginal people and their communities, the more I think that they have got it right in regard to the importance of their way of life. It is all family-based, and we in the Western world are the ones that need the changing of how we live, not the other way around.

I finish by saying how much joy and heartfelt wonder I and the Footys4All family have had through the Footys4All journey so far. I challenge you, the reader, to find your very own Footys4All journey in helping someone not as fortunate as yourself, and I guarantee you it will provide you with a feeling that no monetary experience in the world can provide for you. It is the feeling that you are making a positive difference in the world, and that my friend, is the feeling of being truly alive.

Thank you for the work you do to bring joy to children who otherwise wouldn't have a chance!! I hope some of these pencils are of some use.

With kindness, Melitta & Beatrice.

PS. Beatrice hopes they enjoy colouring in as much as she does!!

CHAPTER 11
Tiffany Pham
(Loc Tho Orphanage)

Tiffany's Story

'It was one big accident, a wonderful one,' is how I respond to being asked about how I started my charity work. Unsurprisingly, nobody ever believes me. I wouldn't believe me either if I had to tell the story to myself.

In 2008 I started to ponder about what I wanted to do when I survived the ten-year milestone in my corporate job in financial services. I didn't have to ponder very long to know what I wanted. It was what all the twenty-something females I knew at the time would have wanted: take a year off; to travel, be a little selfish, and enjoy life. Yes, that thought extended to staying in luxurious hotels and dining in Michelin star restaurants in the world's iconic cities…and possibly buying a few pairs of sky-high stilettos here and there. Ok, maybe many-many pairs of stilettos. You get the picture.

My year off work would commence in October 2009, concluding in September 2010 and I thoroughly enjoyed the meticulous planning for the approaching momentous occasion, especially going to the

Vancouver Winter Olympic Games and the World Cup Soccer in South Africa in 2010.

My round the world airfare was already booked by the time my year-long vacation started in October 2009. My intention was to spend one month at home, saying farewells before departing in November 2009. And one thing got in the way of those very simple plans. My mum.

Mum is one of nine children and many of her siblings left post-war Vietnam in 1975, seeking refugee status in countries such as Australia, France, and the Netherlands. I was born in Nha Trang on Vietnam's south coast where my parents are from, and my family were fortunate to be sponsored to leave Vietnam thanks to relatives who had settled in Brisbane, Australia. So as a little toddler with both my parents, I arrived off a Qantas plane to a new home, Brisbane.

Growing up in my first seven years of life, I was an only child and spent five of those seven years in suburban Brisbane (before moving to Melbourne) without many Vietnamese people in the community. I was brought up like any other Aussie kid. My parents worked a lot, trying to make a comfortable life in their new home. So, after school I was always next door at the neighbour's house playing with the two sisters who were around my age. Sylvia and Annabelle.

I remember we were a bit tom-boy-ish, making mud pies, climbing, and falling off fences and out of trees – I always had scrapes and was very clumsy. I was at my neighbour's so often that I ate there quite a bit and became accustomed to a Western palate – especially drowning eggs on toast with tomato sauce and lathering toast with thick black vegemite. I still do that to this day! For a Vietnamese kid, you can say that I wasn't very Vietnamese at all.

Back to my year-long vacation and my mum who desperately wanted me to go to Vietnam, even for a bit she pleaded before I embarked on my round the world trip – which she knew very well, would not include Vietnam (much to her dismay). After all, I had been to Singapore, Bali,

Thailand, Malaysia and Hong Kong…and ignorantly thought Vietnam would just be…well…kind of the same. After all, it was in Asia, hot, humid, and tropical.

I never had any interest in going to Vietnam, the thought never crossed my mind. I didn't even like Vietnamese food – there were just too many components of food served on multiple plates or in multiple bowls, often spicy and you had to share the food. I did not like spicy food. My level of spice would be the lemon and herb marinade option for burgers at Nandos. I preferred my meal all on one plate – with a knife and fork.

I also did not know the language well. Despite my parent's best endeavours to nurture and cultivate me into a well-rounded Vietnam-ese kid, it just was not happening for me. I did not have any Vietnam-ese friends. And I am sure they were both embarrassed and ashamed of me when I failed Vietnamese Saturday school at the tender age of eight years old.

I completely put it down to the fact that I only understood the Viet-namese that was spoken at home, simple everyday Vietnamese words, and in the southern dialect and accent that I was used to hearing my parents, three siblings, and some relatives speak…but if they spoke too fast – they may as well have spoken Martian! I tried to learn Vietnamese again in high school in grade nine and the Vietnamese teacher actually told me to pick another language to learn!

After consistent nagging by mum, I finally gave in and decided to visit the motherland for two weeks in mid-October 2009. I bought a Vietnam travel guide and literally did everything it recommended at the higher end as far as budget and comfort goes. I packed three suitcases and a cabin bag for my 10-day trip, bringing with me seven bathing suits, five pairs of stilettos, and three big floppy beach hats. I did not own flat shoes back then – aside from flip-flops. I did not eat street or hawker style food. I only used bottled water, even to clean my feet if they got dirty from wearing flip flops – much to the absolute disgust of the locals who witnessed me in this act. I had so much to learn.

While in Nha Trang, the travel guide recommended dining at a restaurant called Lanterns as it was (and still is) highly rated. It looked safe and clean, so I gave it a go. The front of their menu stated that by dining there, patrons were also supporting three local orphanages. Orphanages? It was such a foreign word to me. The first orphanage the restaurant supported was a Catholic one in the city, where (I was told by the wait staff) they get support from the Catholic Church as well as many worshippers and tourists – because it is in the city. The second was Long Son Pagoda, a Buddhist place of worship which was also in the city and got quite a bit of support from the busloads of tourists descending there every day. I knew this because I was one of those tourists on one of those tour buses. The third was Loc Tho Pagoda, Orphanage and Charity School ('Loc Tho'); the only detail provided was that it was in the *'village side'*.

The menu also stated that the restaurant could arrange visits to any of the orphanages if patrons were interested in helping. I asked the wait staff, of the three orphanages, which was the poorest? I was told it was Loc Tho. I then asked for the address, so I could arrange for a driver to take me. The response I got was a *'no'*, followed by an explanation that there is no address and it was simply *'in the village'*, that it was *'too far away'*, and there was *'nothing to do there'*, and tried persuading me to visit the city establishments instead.

I insisted that I would really like to see Loc Tho because it seemed they needed the most help and I honestly did not believe Loc Tho had 'no address' – such things just simply did not exist in my sheltered brain. Every building, structure, location has an address! I persisted with trying to get an address, so I could make my own way there.

Then I was told that even locals living in the city did not know of Loc Tho's existence, that only those who know about it - know how to get there. This intensified my curiosity. I managed to convince the staff member to take me there and I would wait for them to finish work and reimburse them for their efforts.

A few hours later, I found myself being guided out of the main tourist district, getting off the main road onto dirt and gravel roads, weaving in and around shanty huts littering little narrow laneways. All of a sudden, we had arrived at Loc Tho...and it only took fifteen minutes when it sounded so far away being *'in the village side.'* I later learnt that to the locals, anything more than a five-minute motor-scooter ride away is considered 'far'. Especially if it's not in the city centre!

I was a little confused and amused when I walked into Loc Tho. It was a surreal feeling, like I had just stepped onto the scene of a Kung-Fu movie – and at any moment now Jackie Chan was going to come flying out doing a side kick through the poorly hammered timber slat buildings!

There was a lot of dirt, rubble, and debris everywhere. It was a dusty eyesore. There were three wooden buildings hammered together with what looked like scavenged pieces of wood and tin. Dirty old torn fabric sheets were nailed to doorways (acting as doors) blowing in the slight breeze.

There were concrete buildings with what looked like flood-stained walls up to about 1.5m. Old nuns in mustard, brown, and grey Buddhist robes were slowly making their way across the grounds, periodically raising their head to acknowledge me – then clasping their hands in a prayer-like motion before slightly bowing their heads and continuing on with whatever they were doing. Kids with dirty faces, dirty-ragged clothing, and shoeless were playing on the gravel, rubble, and dirt ground. Then there were other kids with the funniest patchy haircuts in miniature Buddhist robes, looking like they belonged in a Jackie Chan movie! It was quite a scene and I did not know what to make of it or how to translate what my eyes were seeing so my brain could process.

My restaurant staffer-guide explained that this place, Loc Tho, is a place for community prayer and worship for the locals as it's a Buddhist pagoda. It is also an orphanage for abandoned kids. That the orphans were the kids with the patchy haircuts in miniature Buddhist robes. They *lived* here. It also served as a charity school. *Yeah, right*...and where exactly is this school? – I asked. I was shown the three wooden buildings hammered together with bits of tin, wood, and sheets of fabric. I was shocked that it was a *'school'*.

I sceptically poked my head in and saw little kids sitting at desks being taught by an older orphan child of fourteen years old. The blackboard was a small piece of tin with the alphabet permanently painted on it. The kids were writing the alphabet and I watched, all the while noticing: the large gaping holes in this 'classroom' and thinking that all manner of things and bugs would come inside when it rained; the unsafe exposed nails and tin sheeting where the kids could so easily hurt themselves; how dusty and dirty it was; and there were no lights or educational visual aids anywhere. Not even a storybook.

It was only when I felt how hot it was under the tin roof that I realised I must have stood in that classroom for at least ten minutes, and some of the kids had not even finished writing the alphabet. I asked the staffer-guide to ask the *'teacher'* what was taking so long and was told that the kids were sharing pencils and had to wait for other classmates to finish. I was speechless.

As I walked around the premises, I saw the young orphans collecting sticks for wood fire to cook with. There was only one small water pump about 30cm off the ground that was used for cooking, cleaning, washing, and bathing. Water from the pump was trickling out very slowly...and the water collected from the pump had a bit of dirt in it. On closer inspection of the kids when they came to say hello, many had all sorts of visible skin sores and open wounds from cuts, abrasions, and infections due to being untreated and uncovered. Some looked malnourished.

There were twelve nuns and fifteen orphans living on site. Additionally, there were about thirty children that walked long distances to attend the charity school, a school that literally had no school resources. Those were my first images of Loc Tho. I did not have any real intention of helping. I was simply curious, and my curiosity was satisfied with the visit.

I was taken back to the restaurant in the tourist district in the city centre after visiting Loc Tho and caught a taxi to the harbour where a speedboat was waiting to take me back to the exclusive private island resort I was staying at.

When I walked into my room, the covers were turned down, chocolates left on my pillows, fresh flowers and fruit on my dresser. There was also a note. A reminder to let the staff know if I would like to have dinner in the restaurant, in my room, on my balcony, or on the sand at the private back beach surrounded by a mini zoo with rare white peacocks wandering around.

I looked around my room. I was paying $US 400 a night, and yet I spent most of the time on a sun bed cooking myself and waiting for the colour of my skin to go from a milky latte to a shade of mocha latte, or I was away from the island – touring the mainland and being absolutely scared to touch anything that looked unsanitary.

I know it sounds clichéd, but that night, buried in the comforts of six pillows, was teary little me. Visions of the children I saw earlier that day kept haunting me. I came to the realisation that it could have been me if my family had not left Vietnam. And I was still being selfish at that moment because I was still thinking of ME.

On my return home, I never told my mother about the visit to Loc Tho. I was still unsure of what it was all supposed to mean. I had one more week at home before departing for my year-long round the world trip. My head and my heart were torn. My head told me that I deserved the year-long trip. I deserved to splurge after quitting university to get a job and keeping my family together after my parents split up. I deserved to splurge for buying my first home at nineteen years old to look after mum and my three younger siblings. I deserved this indulgent break. My heart was telling me, that all those children I saw were an extension of my younger siblings, and that they too, needed a big sister to look after them.

Time was not a problem. I had a lot of spare time…over eleven months to be exact. Money was not the problem either. I had planned and saved for this trip. Saved to simply blow the money on what would have been less meaningful experiences, only to be remembered and depicted in photos I took, or stories I would tell, or blown on material purchases that I did not need, which I would either eventually wear out or would have thrown out.

There was nothing fundamentally stopping me from going back to Vietnam. Nothing at all. The next day I cashed in my round the world ticket and bought a one-way ticket back to Vietnam.

I had no idea what volunteering actually entailed so I signed up to a Vietnam volunteering program with an NGO based out of New Zealand which had programs in Africa, Asia, and South America. I was assigned to volunteer in a town called Tam Ky – in central Vietnam near the coast (about an hour south of Hoi An) with eight other volunteers from Australia, Finland, Canada, Chile, and the United States.

Some volunteers were on a two-week placement and up to one month. I was there for three months. Our efforts to help orphans, disadvantaged young children and teenagers, and severely disabled children cost us $US 500 in a once off program joining fee, and $US2,000 a month. We were told the cost would cover accommodation, all home cooked meals, transport to the different placements and a program leader who also acted as a guide and translator.

The accommodation was a very run down, unkept, and un-hygienic three-bedroom two-storey house on the main road. There was damp rising on the walls, cockroaches, rats, flies, mosquitos, spiders, and graffiti on the walls in some of the bedrooms from previous volunteers. The home cooked meals were prepared in the unhygienic damp rising kitchen and were very basic meals. The transportation was not very reliable, and we had to often walk to placement or cycle on unsafe bicycles where the brakes would not work, the handlebars were stiff – not turning properly - or the chain continually came off.

I had to share with a volunteer from Finland, and our 'room' was an open family room upstairs and our beds were two disgusting flimsy single mattresses on the floor that were riddled with bed bugs (I still have scars on my legs from the bites) and a dusty mosquito net with gaping holes.

I stood in that room paralysed at what I was seeing, overwhelmed with emotion, I started to sob. This is not what I had expected. What the hell had I done? My roommate from Finland was equally as appalled (but held it together much better than I did) and gave me an encouraging hug.

Meeting the children that we were going to help at the orphanage (children from new born to eleven years old), Home of Affection (orphaned children from four to seventeen years old) and the disabled children's hospital (children of all ages) put it all into perspective and I never once complained again about the condition of the volunteers' accommodation, the food, or transport – or lack of.

For five out of the seven days in the week, volunteers would teach children English, arts and craft, play sports and games, feed the kids, and provide some kind of mental and physical stimulation for the babies and the disabled children. All these placements were affiliated with the government and therefore NGO charity organisations were able to establish programs.

I was very naïve to think that the money volunteers paid to help would actually go to the placements and the children. Very naïve indeed.

We quickly learnt that not a cent of what we paid went to where it really needed to go. The carers at the baby orphanage kept telling us there was not enough food, milk, nappies, clothes, or medicine for the children – asking us to help. Volunteers used their own money and continued to buy and replenish stock on a weekly basis. The Home of Affection was the same. There was not enough food, clothes, educational books, blankets, pillows, etc. Again, volunteers continued to buy supplies. At the disabled children's hospital, volunteers bought food and interactive learning aids and mobility aids to help the children.

Between the six volunteers we would have paid over $US 10,000 in those three months. Where did all the money go? Certainly not to the kids. During those three months I learnt so much. The women who cared for the children at the baby orphanage were paid equivalent to $AUD 80 per month. Renting a fully furnished three-storey home was about $AUD 300 per month and the average salary was $AUD 1,200 a year. So where did all that money go?

I repetitively asked the director of the Vietnam volunteering program about the unaccounted money and was never given an actual response. He didn't even try. I wrote to the NGO headquarters in New Zealand detailing my concerns and never heard back. So, I left the program just two weeks shy of my three-month tenure there. Turns out I was not the first or the only volunteer to have voiced such concerns and strangely enough, one year later that Vietnam volunteering program did not continue.

One positive thing that came from that first Vietnam volunteering experience was what I learnt as far as the culture in Vietnam and how far the dollar goes. The best thing was being so fortunate to have met and nursed the dozen babies at the baby orphanage. After I left, I found out that all the babies got adopted to families in Spain and to this day I remain in contact with the children and their families, even travelling to Spain twice to reunite with them all.

When I left Tam Ky, I did not know what to do next. So, I headed back to the only other city I was most familiar with – Nha Trang – with absolutely no plans. So, one day, as a bored tourist, I thought I would go back and visit Loc Tho and see if there was anything I could do there. The Head Nun was pleasant enough, but she did not give me any indication that she wanted my help or that there was anything that they specifically needed me to do. Nothing. I was told that I could do bits here and there. Not a whole lot of interest or direction from the nuns at all. But I wasn't put off by it.

So, every day I went to Loc Tho from 9am to 5pm. Even on the weekends. In Vietnam school runs from 7am – 4pm and is six days a week, including Saturdays. It is normal for school children to leave the school at lunchtime and go home for lunch and have a nap before class resumes at 2pm. However, the children from the neighbouring villages attending the charity school did not go home. They stayed on site, had lunch and had a nap. The reason for this is that the children lived far away and may not come back to school. Also, there was a high probability that nobody would be home and they would not have anything to eat. So, the nuns kept them at school.

I would still go to Loc Tho on a Sunday as it was a good way to see the 'domestic' side of Loc Tho with none of the poor charity school kids in attendance. I spent the first few weeks just observing the daily operations of the 'school', the pagoda as a place of worship and as a home for the nuns and the orphans. And instinctively, I started to buy urgent supplies.

Firstly, baby supplies. There were three orphaned babies at birth who were under the age of eleven months. On this particular afternoon when I was bottle-feeding, I had one in my arms, one lying on my lap and the other was swaying on in a makeshift hammock. Out of the corner of my eye, I could see flies on top of some milk bottle teats and tried to swat them – but the flies would not move. Gross! I thought – they must be

99

dead flies. Ewww! After my baby duties were done, I grabbed the teats and on closer inspection they were not flies at all – much to my relief. Curiously, the teats were stitched with black thread which gave the impression there were files on it. I took the teats and asked one of the nuns why they were stitched. I was told that the older babies were teething and with their gums itching they were biting the teats – creating bigger holes. And when the younger babies were being feed, they would choke from the rapid milk flow. So, they stitched the holes.

I naively asked why you don't just buy new teats? The response was 'we cannot afford to buy them'. I thought to myself – how much could they possibly be?! Turns out that a two-pack was only thirty cents, so I bought a dozen of them! Then there were the nappies, well, lack of. The nappies used were two handkerchiefs. One folded into a rectangle and placed inside one that is folded as a triangle. Not very absorbent at all! So, I bought nappies. And then there was the 'milk' that was being fed to the babies, which was the residue liquid from making steamed rice. And with that, I bought tins of proper baby milk formula. To help with hydration and lack of other nutrients, I started bottle-feeding the babies with soluble hydrolytes and multivitamins. They gained a healthy amount of weight only a few weeks later.

So many of the children were sick. Stomach aches, malnutrition, cuts, insect bites, topical skin infections, ring worms, scabies, lice, fevers, and the list went on. There were days when I would see children with horrible swelling to parts of their face and limbs from insect bites – even from a scorpion. Other days there were children hobbling around with leaves or scraps of material packed on their limbs held together by an elastic band with dried blood visually seen around the *'treated'* area.

So, I started a lunch time first aid health check program. Every day after the children had their lunch and before they had an afternoon nap, they would come see me on the neighbouring bench where lunch was served so I could do visual mouth, nose, eye, ears, and skin inspections and treat them as best I could. It took some weeks before the children were brave enough and trusted me enough to come to me and tell me about their pain.

I later learnt that the equipment I sprawled out on the bench scared them (scissors, tweezers, probing needles, bottles of unfamiliar solution, and ointments, etc.). I also learnt that these children often had to look after themselves and did not get any affection or care from anyone, so it was very difficult for them to have trust in a stranger to treat and care for them. So as the weeks went by, more and more children came to see me. Then the nuns came to see me. And so, the first aid and medical treatment program began.

Additional water pumps were installed around the premises, arising from a harrowing and horrible burn accident. It was during lunch one afternoon when one of the nuns was carrying a metal bucket full of hot soup from the kitchen to the dining hall. A little three-year-old girl attending the charity school accidently turned around when the nun behind her was lifting the bucket onto the table. I will never forget the violent screams that ensued from that little girl. She was completely doused in seven litres of hot soup.

There was so much yelling and screaming from the nuns and the children that I completely froze for a second. Some people rushed to the only water pump that was about 40m away with bowls to collect water and trying their hardest to cool her down. It was a completely fruitless exercise, so I carried her to the pump and cradled her head as she lay under the water trickling out of the pump.

That was the first time I cried at Loc Tho.

She was sobbing hysterically from the immense pain. I was crying because as the water trickled over her, I could see the effects of the burn. Her face, eyelids, ears, neck, shoulders, and chest started to swell, blister and char, and I felt I failed her, because I could not keep her cool enough without decent running water. When she seemed cooled enough and after she dried off, I took her into one of the nun's private quarters and applied cooling cream all over her. I stayed with her, fanning her while she slept and although she had stopped crying, I was still crying because I felt completely helpless. What could I, a Vietnamese born westerner (known by locals as a Viet Kieu) possibly know about the hardships these people and children face? How could I even begin to imagine what their life is really like and to help?

When her mother came to pick her up the child did not want to let go of me and was smiling at me despite what she had endured. Seeing her little girl covered in white ointment, her mother demanded the nuns explain what happened, and progressed to screaming at the nuns for not looking after her daughter, that she trusted her daughter's welfare to the nuns and now her little girl's face was mangled, and nobody would ever want to marry her.

It was heart-breaking to see how the nuns were treated and the anguish the mother felt and the fear in the little girl's face as she left with her mother. I am pleased to say that through daily treatment of her wounds, there was absolutely no scarring and the little girl is now in her final year of primary school at the charity school and is a beautiful darling girl.

I started to teach a few English classes and found it extremely difficult with my limited Vietnamese and absolutely no supplies. So, I created my own teaching supplies. Creating visual flash cards and teaching aids in both English and Vietnamese (translated by local friends I had met), so the children knew how to count, say the English alphabet (I learnt the Vietnamese alphabet did not contain 'F', 'J' 'W' and 'Z'), days of the week, months of year, the seasons, everyday objects, conversational English sentences, and nursery rhymes. All these were printed, laminated, and stuck up in the classroom. The friends I had met were fascinated with what I was doing and as they had never heard of Loc Tho, they would often come out on their days off to help me.

So my daily routine was: getting to Loc Tho at 9am; checking on everyone to see how they were; help feed the little children (cos they eat so slow and must eat what may be their only meal for the day); help get the little kids to nap; set up and serve lunch to the older kids; perform medical first aid treatment; have lunch; tend to the babies; prepare class lesson plans; teach English classes; go place orders/buy supplies; have an early dinner; respond to all the queries I was getting from family, friends and colleagues; and do it all over again. Every day.

For months in the back of my mind, one thing kept me awake at night. It was the timber classrooms. So, I spoke to the Head Nun (via a friend translating) about building a new proper classroom. She was hesitant because she did not know how they would manage the upkeep of the classroom. This included fitting it out with a blackboard, table and chairs, school supplies, a proper teacher, etc.

I told her that building the classroom would include all of that – I wasn't going to build a shell of a classroom and leave it up to them to figure the rest out. She then asked whether with the new classroom they could bring in more children from the village who have been on the waiting list. And I said 'of course'! I had no idea there was even a waiting list (to this day there is still a waiting list). Knowing what she was thinking, I reassured her that we would be able to feed and look after all the current and new children too. I did not know exactly how I was going to do it, or how much it would even cost – but I was determined, and it was going to happen. No matter what.

I was prepared to get my siblings to sell my BMW motorcar at home to pay for the classroom. The Head Nun was so pleased she actually took my hands in hers and bowed her head to me. I didn't know what this meant. My friend later explained that Buddhist nuns do not show much emotion or affection and what I got was one huge amount of affection from this frail nun. I later learnt that the only reason why the Head Nun trusted that I was going to do what I said was because aside from the charity school children and the residents, I was the only person who continued to come every day to help; that I was implementing programs for the benefit of the children; that the children adored me and the nuns adored me; that she was watching me like a hawk every day to see what this Viet Kieu was doing. And that she was beginning to trust me.

A few days later I met with the architect and builders and trades people. It was happening so fast! And I found out that things can happen really quick in Vietnam. The classroom would be a double sized classroom which could hold thirty students comfortably. It would have a new adjoining bathroom block. The blackboard would be ordered from the city (Nha Trang city), the tables and chairs would be constructed by a local tradesman (who happened to live a few doors down from Loc Tho). All the trades people would cease work on their other jobs and focus entirely on building the new classroom. That it would take five weeks with them working from first light to last light – seven days a week. And it would cost me $AUD 10,000.

$10,000? Are you sure? I had to ask (thinking back to a few years prior where I spent over $AUD 5,000 on snow apparel before I had even seen the snow!). The architect and builder asked if I thought it was too much, because they were giving me everything at almost cost, donating their time with the architectural drawings and surveying the site.

They even told me that the trades people are hardly getting paid because they live near Loc Tho and have so much respect for what Loc Tho does for the community – so in essence they were also volunteering their time to work before 7am, after 7pm, and on Sundays. I was even told that the trades people would provide life time maintenance of the classroom for free. I was also told that the only immediate funds needed was to buy the materials to lay the foundation and that I could pay everything else at the end.

They had so much trust in me and I was still shocked. When I had digested everything, I thanked them and told them I would pay them in three intervals because I did not want anyone to be out of pocket during construction. That afternoon, heavy machinery rolled in and excavation began to the absolute amazement of the children.

As soon as I got back to my budget $USD 4 a night accommodation (don't be alarmed – it was not dodgy and I was very comfortable with air conditioning, satellite television and free Wi-Fi), I spread the word to my network of contacts that I was planning to build a new classroom. The offers of help started to flood in. It was such an exciting time for everyone at Loc Tho.

Since then I have built a further two double sized classrooms, with all children now in uniforms. There is a full complement of classes from pre-school, kindergarten, and grade one through to grade five (the highest level in primary school).

The charity school now has over one hundred and forty children, and teachers in each class. There is a high-school scholarship program. There is a dedicated room full of education books and school supplies for the children. There is a well-stocked proper infirmary with Western medicine to treat the children and adjoining herbal medicine room and two nurses staffing it, where treatment has now expanded to treating the poor people in the local village free of charge.

There are weather-resistant stone tables and benches around the premises for the children to sit on. There are herb and vegetable gardens. A formal cultural and educational immersion program has been in place for the last six years with grade six students from a private school in Western Victoria, Australia. The private school students join in every facet of the daily school activities at Loc Tho, including feeding the little ones and setting up and serving lunch to the older children.

I go over every September for two to three weeks with a group of volunteers who have sought me out and they do exactly everything I do (except all the paper work) to get a real 'hands-on, grass-roots' experience of what it is like to volunteer aboard. Volunteers pay their own airfares and accommodation. There are no program joining fees or placement fees. What I do is 100% purpose-led charity work.

Not a cent is spent on any administration or overhead costs — because there aren't any. Volunteers raise money to bring over to buy local supplies to pay for certain programs. Others may bring over supplies that are not easily available or are considered a luxury item and very expensive (e.g. children's multivitamins, baby bibs, gauze, bandages, latex gloves, educational visual aids, and picture story books, etc.).

Over the course, of a year, I get many people asking if they can visit Loc Tho — even when I am not there. And I help facilitate this. There are no mandatory requirements. You don't need to be a teacher, or a doctor. You just need to be a compassionate human being with the want to help, and I will find a way for you to help within the realms of your comfort zone and our ability. My youngest volunteers were 18 months old and they helped in the pre-school class with the alphabet, counting, and nursery rhymes. There is always something for anyone who wants to help.

My mum was in total shock when she learnt about what I got up to on my year off. She did not believe me, or anyone who told her about my charity work. She did not believe that her eldest daughter, who did not understand the culture, customs or speak Vietnamese fluently could survive in Vietnam on her own for that long or be capable of doing anything other than go shopping or sunbathe.

Despite seeing all the photos, she simply did not believe it. A few years after I returned from my year-long trip, mum went back to Vietnam — only her second time since she left. She went to Loc Tho and spoke to the Head Nun about me. Still she did not believe it. Mum saw the plaques on the classroom with my name on it, and the donated stone benches with my siblings' names on it, and still did not believe it. She showed the Head Nun a photo of me and asked the Head Nun if she was certain it was me who had been there for the year and helped them. The Head Nun said yes. I think mum believes me now.

I am not a registered charity, not an NGO, or a not-for-profit organisation. And primarily due to this, I do not have the financial backing of any companies or corporations or wealthy individuals bequeathing their funds onto me (due to tax implications). I have people who have seen me completely transform and mature in life's purpose over the last decade, and it is these people who are my supporters. Even more so, many of these people were strangers at first – sceptical, who over the years could not deny how Loc Tho has transformed, and these strangers have become good friends. Some are even dedicated volunteers who go over every year.

These days I rarely wear stilettos. The only enjoyment I get out of shopping is when I find cheap discounted multivitamins that I can buy in bulk for the children or other supplies needed that are on sale. I can travel for weeks with only the flip-flops on my feet and a backpack as carry on. The executive sports BMW I loved was sold with proceeds going towards the children. The material possessions I own are far less than what it was, and yet it is more fulfilling.

I now love Vietnamese food and have such a greater appreciation for the culture, customs, the resilience of my people and hard times faced by so many. I owe nothing to Vietnam as Australia is my home. I am proud to be Australian and I would not live anywhere other than Australia. Vietnam is where I was born. It's in my blood and it will forever be in my heart.

When I say to people that my blood, sweat, and tears have gone into creating a better place for these children, I really do mean it. In my first year I was doing it all on my own. I didn't have time to eat or sleep. My immune system was compromised because I was constantly surrounded by children who were so sick.

I eventually contracted whooping cough and pneumonia at the same time, coughing for six weeks and even coughed up blood. I was hospitalised in Nha Trang. My travel insurance company was put on notice and after receiving medical reports, I was given five days to leave and come home or my insurance policy would be cancelled. I guess my condition was much more serious than I allowed myself to believe it was. I had dropped from a healthy 46kgs to a frail 38kgs. So, I came home.

My lung function was severely impacted. I went from someone who was a fit and healthy black belt in taekwondo, who could run in stilettos, to someone who could not even walk ten metres without puffing and panting in flat shoes. I suffered two respiratory seizures in the first two weeks when I came home and as a result I have low lung function in my right lung. I still suffer from the effects of low lung function today.

It is now almost twenty years that I have been in the same corporate workplace where much of my income supplements the running costs of Loc Tho. Today, as with every other day for the past nine years, with constant good food, improved nutrition, education programs/supplies, medical care, and infrastructure, there are now one hundred and sixty children at Loc Tho. All are happy. All are healthy. All have a better chance in life. And that is my story. All I did was have the will to help, and I found a way to do it. And strangers can be truly wonderful.

From Tiffany's volunteers:

'From the moment we first arrived at Loc Tho it was clear that this was a special place. The nuns and people there embraced us as though we were part of the family. The first moment we met the kids it was obvious that this culture ran throughout. My sons are both tall and had children climbing on them and asking to be picked up...Each night after dinner Tiffany would collect the leftover food from the restaurants we ate at as a volunteer group and handed them out to people living on the streets. My two sons became part of this nightly ritual...On arriving in Vietnam I was nervous about how my youngest son Bayley would cope. He at the time was very quiet and not very open to new experiences. From the moment we

first arrived at Loc Tho and he had children climbing on him and had no choice but to be drawn in to their open and fun-loving ways. He now is a confident fun loving outgoing young man and I have no doubt that his experience in Vietnam was the start of this...We were going for a holiday and some volunteer work. My intention was to give to the community as a family. What I got was far beyond my expectations. For all of us it was life-changing. When I went there I thought it was so nice that Tiffany did this charity work and helped these people in another part of the world. I now realise that it doesn't end there. Tiffany has not only enriched and changed the life of the people of Loc Tho, but she also enriched the lives of many around her. Her attitude to life is infectious and inspirational. My student has most definitely become my teacher.'

~ Scott

'Tiffany's charity work first came to my attention when she selflessly pulled out of a well-deserved twelve month around the world trip in order to create a better life and future for less fortunate children from her homeland...Tiffany wanted to create an environment for orphans and children in one of the poorer areas of Nha Trang that would see them have at least some chance to learn and grow... Without any backing or experience, she began to raise funds for basic things as medicines, first aid supplies, books, stationery, and other educational resources as well as class rooms...Tiffany has also been able to secure donations to allow some of the children to continue on to high school...I donated for several years and finally went over to Nha Trang in 2015 as part of the volunteer group...I have been every year since and it is the highlight of my year... Tiffany is a powerhouse when it comes to her charity work and what she has done, a true Humanitarian Rockstar.'

~ Grant

'*Tiffany is a whirlwind and if you sit still for long enough she will pick you up and bring you along on the vortex. A few years ago, I heard about Tiffany and the work she was doing for an orphanage & charity school in Vietnam. I arranged to visit the orphanage with Tiffany as I was interested to see how donation funds were being used. I saw how the funds raised help the children and also the community. The orphans and another one hundred and thirty children from the community would not have the opportunity to get an education if it wasn't for Tiffany's charity work. The majority of funds raised are used to run the school, from building & maintaining classrooms, paving play areas, teachers' salaries, down to the pencils and paper and most importantly a healthy meal (which for some children will be the only meal of the day). The sharing of the experience with a school from Australia is beneficial to children of both countries. Tiffany doesn't proclaim to know it all & willingly takes advice on ways to benefit the children. A classic example is reading glasses – seven children now have reading glasses. Another is sponsoring children to extend to high school. She'll canvas her loyal following and others to raise funds for whatever needs doing. My team at work have run a number of fundraisers and what's great is that we are able to see where our funds are being used. I think the difference with Tiffany is that integrity is everything. Making sure those dollars raised are used to benefit the children, which unfortunately isn't always the case with some charities. We are privileged to play an important role in the care of these children and I'm grateful that I was caught up in the vortex.*'

– Jennifer

'The excitement on the faces of the nuns and children when Tiffany arrived brought tears to our eyes…Consulting with the nuns to make sure that the most needed items were purchased first and seeing 100% of all money raised going straight to Loc Tho is heart-warming and fulfilling…The care and organisation that goes into the volunteer trips organised by Tiffany is outstanding to say the least, and it has allowed us to meet the most beautiful people and fulfil some of our dreams of helping people not as lucky as us to get an education and for some, their only meal of the day. Tiffany – you are a wonderful person, with way, way too much energy and a heart of gold and we are honoured to be able to help you with your continued work with the Loc Tho.'

– Brendon & Rachel

Such a brilliant and simple idea that can help thousands of children around the world. Amazing! Laura x

CHAPTER 12
The Mainstayers and Mentors

As the Pencils Community evolves, it reminds me of a river. Sometimes flowing gently around rocks and obstacles and then suddenly we are in the rushing water, trying to keep up. There are many bends in the river and we meet so many wonderful people as we paddle along. Wonderful humanitarians like the ones you have just read about.

Throughout all the twists and turns and the river breaking off into many tributaries, there are the core group of people that I speak with daily. These are the people where the Skype calls are done long into the night or the early morning calls over breakfast, asking for advice or direction on something that is happening. This is my key group that I run ideas past and have them check in on me to make sure I am not saying 'YES' to everything…which is what I do. Those people are Ocean, my Mum, Oli, and Val.

'You are the toughest chick I know,' laughs Ocean on the other end of the phone.

I am relaying to him some latest story and drama. I ask him, 'What if I am too sick to do the presentation? I mean we really had better come up with a contingency plan.'

'Like what do you mean, if you are too sick?' he says. 'Give me some examples.'

'I don't know,' I pause. Unsure of what to say. 'What if I am in hospital or something, you know how this shit can just go pear-shaped overnight…and I'd be in another country!' I wonder if he has thought about this too. I know Ocean so well that it would have crossed his mind at least once, but he would never say anything.

He has seen me present to groups under some hellish conditions. Like when I first started Methotrexate, (*Methotrexate is a low dose chemo medication that was given to me in the hope it would suppress my immune system and slow the arthritis down*). It affected me badly, and prior to a presentation with Ocean I disappeared for a few minutes to go outside and vomit on the nature strip. I came in and did my presentation to a standing ovation. He didn't know until I told him afterwards. He gave me serious grief for not telling him.

Since then I have made a deal with him to always be 100% transparent about my health, to which his normal response is 'Yep' or 'So?' It sounds cold but it's not. He knows if I get to my limit then I will tell him, and he is one of the few people that doesn't treat me as 'sick'. He knows that there are so many other aspects to who I am, who I was before this life-chapter, and who I will be going forward. He and his gorgeous wife Vicki Jane have always had my back. I love them dearly.

So, I say again, 'You know, hospital. What's our backup plan?'

In his cheerful and animated voice, he yells down the phone, 'Well we will just have to cross live to you in the hospital to do your presentation there!' He laughs because he knows I would too.

'But I look rubbish in white!' I say protesting and laughing at the same time!

'Put a Pencils t-shirt on over the top of your hospital gown then!'

But then he adds in a more serious tone, 'Rockstar I've got your back, I'll sort it if I need to.' And just like that, there is the reassurance I was looking for.

For many years, my surname 'Rochstein' has long since been replaced with the alternative, 'Rockstar'- which I find amusing as it has happened in many different circles, so it must be what sticks as a nick-name.

It's hard to put into words my feelings for Ocean. He is more than a friend and mentor – he has seen me from my days as a 'green' writer, fresh from the vine and having no clues. He has laughed at my stories of picking my first proof book up off the nature strip as the pages flew out, me on my knees scrambling about for the pages and crying, 'This isn't my dream.' (I thought I hadn't read the fine print and paid enough money to have my book glued together and Ocean tried his best to contain his laughter as he explained to me that a proof copy is supposed to look like that, so you can read through it and make changes easier). He encouraged me next time to not be so dramatic as I opened the envelope containing my proof copy! Luckily, I got to open proof letters another four times with my subsequent published books.

Over the years we have travelled and presented together, he has been my rock and I know I have been his too. Keeping my opinions direct and also no bullshit has meant that he always gets an honest and raw account, and so do I – it works both ways. Do I think he's an absolute legend and sage – of course I do. But I keep it real for him as he does me.

I recall at one presentation I was changing my introduction last minute. He leans over to me and quietly whispers in a slow powerful, deep voice, 'Remember who you are…'

He caught me off guard and all I could imagine at this point was 'Mufasa from the Lion King' as that is what Mufasa says to Simba (his lion cub) when he is a ghost in the sky.

Dumbfounded, I turn to Ocean and said somewhat confused, 'What, Simba the lion?' and we both fell about laughing.

This is our sense of humour and whenever we are working together or hanging out it is always a time of fun and pure joy. That and we work twenty-three hours a day! I always come home from a trip from

Queensland, empowered and inspired, inevitably with a new book outline which has been written at the airport, or a new marketing plan thought out and I return home very much in need of some sleep.

The difference is that along the journey I have evolved to become on a more equal platform with him – but he has done that for me; he has created the space for me in which to grow. He has encouraged me to step up and out of my skin, he has forced me to learn skills I otherwise would not, and he has let some skills go, giving up on things like my coloured Excel spreadsheets and work flow management. His desk is impeccable, his email in-tray neatly organised and answered and filed away.

My desk is a shambles; piles of books and laptops balancing precariously on tissue boxes or breakfast plates. One of us is chaos and the other is not but we are both true to our creative process and for that I am grateful to have been nurtured along the way.

Ocean's wife, Vicki-Jane is the 'yin' to Ocean's 'yang'. Yin refers to femininity and the trough of a wave (Vicki-Jane), whilst yang (Ocean) refers to brightness, passion and growth. Vicki, has long been the other supporter of me. She allows me the space to be 'female' in the moment and honest, raw, vulnerable and emotional at times. She gives me perspective and is as tough and authentic as they come. In many ways she reminds me of Bela from OrphFund with her 'No Bullshit' approach also. I reflect on the fact that these are the type of women I attract in my life and I am eternally grateful to them all.

Vicki-Jane helps keep me focused and on my path by helping me keep it real. She is the creative 'ideas' woman because she has intuition behind her. She is extremely in touch with her emotions and has a unique power within her and can see the things (or obstacles) that stand in my way, even if I cannot. She is my marketing guru, telling me about harnessing my inner power as a woman, as a writer and as a humanitarian... and she is my long-time friend.

Without Ocean and Vicki's support it would be a much harder journey and certainly one that wasn't as fun! They are my family. Now we have a team on board with our #CanoeFleet and they all provide valuable insight and perspective into Pencils. Coupled with the legendary, 'Val' I feel we have a winning and dynamic team that come to Pencils from the right place, a place of love.

I can't go on and talk about love and not talk about my Mum, my daughter, and my sister. When Pencils continued to grow, they were the first ones to back me and come on board as Directors. We make a great team. And they also know that this is my legacy to Olive, my gorgeous little girl who is growing so fast. And they are helping me achieve this.

It sounds very flat and morbid, but it isn't. We all have an expiry date; mine is just a bit more commonly talked about and I am pretty open about it, especially with Mum. I can't imagine it's easy for her to hear in any way, but she listens and hides her pain. She watches me do things that take longer than they should, like chop up vegetables and yet she sits patiently, has a wine, and listens. There is a rare strength in that, that makes me feel she is the strongest woman on earth.

Mum's life hasn't always been easy. She has become tough over the years because she has learnt to be. She is a woman of morals and integrity; she is fierce, and yet gentle and encouraging. She is fitter and stronger than me physically and many others and she is always positive. She has to watch her youngest sister and her youngest daughter fight the same disease. It must feel cruel for her to have to witness this, but she keeps on keeping on. She helps in any way she can, and I see her every week and speak with her a few times in the week. We are very close.

My older sister has her own busy life, a doctor, married to a doctor, and five children. She is extremely hard working and driven, yet when I need her, like truly need her – she is there in a heartbeat. When I need guidance, she gives me both a medical opinion and a sisterly opinion. I love seeing her and the kids; it always seems like there is never enough time. I guess that's because how it feels when you are with the ones you love, that there never is enough time.

On the other side of the world, my brother gives me great advice, business advice on how to build. He has taught me to operate from my gut instinct and he has the same drive I have, his for his business and mine for the charity sector. I run big scale ideas past him and his tenacity has taught me how to survive and grow Pencils Community on no money, just creative ideas. He was the one who taught me the concept of bootstrapping and doing everything for yourself. He taught me about weighing up risk and making really hard business decisions without emotion – something that is very difficult for me, but as Pencils evolves so to do I as a leader.

And then there is my Dad, always dubious in the beginning and then his curiosity got the better of him. I think the concept of Pencils appealed to him; he was once a primary school teacher in the country (I even encouraged him to write a book on his time as a young teacher, teaching children of all ages in a singular classroom back in the 1960s). Dad now gets up and sings my praises at his local Probus Group meetings and encourages members to donate. There is often a box of pencils for me at the door when I go to visit him.

But as a mother, I think this is where I have learnt one of my greatest roles. Especially as a single mum, independence and tenacity became my survival skills. I have a daughter to raise and to teach well. So, for the past decade, it's really just been Olive and me. She is sweet, smart, and funny and I like to think that I have had something to do with this!

When I was young, about 16 years old, I remember having this vivid memory or rather a vision. In the vision, it was very sepia in colour, but I was older, perhaps fifty odd:

I am squatting down next to a teenage girl (perhaps this was my future vision of Olive). We are squatting on the edge of a small embankment. It is very dusty and dirty; it looks like sand and dried mud, like a ditch. We are doing something with our hands, looking at bracelets or beading perhaps. I feel like we are somewhere overseas, Africa or Asia perhaps but I can't tell. I feel like we are dressed in lovely colourful fabrics, a bit hippie-looking and we are both smiling and laughing gently. I wonder if that vision will one day become real and I will look back and go 'Hahhh, I did see it,' or perhaps I am manifesting it all along, willing it to happen. Perhaps we are somewhere on a journey together with Pencils. Who knows, I'll let you know if it happens!

My gorgeous girl is now nine years old. She is unique and immense all at the same time, and I adore her. I am spending a great deal more of my time with her at present. Last year we decided to home-school Oli for a variety of reasons, but the main one being that traditional school wasn't working out for her. It was when we were travelling with Pencils in August 2017 in Tasmania for a pilot-project and desperately trying to keep up with her schoolwork that we realised that without the pressure of formal schooling, she actually loved learning. This was as much as a surprise to me too! It's fair to say we had spent many a school morning in the driveway or me sitting on the play equipment until mid-morning – only to get a call an hour later to come and pick her up. I even got so used to it that I would take a notebook and write while I sat on the childlike seats at the garden at her school. Needless to say, my little girl is much happier now.

We trialled fourth term of home-schooling, figuring it was just like a parent taking their kids out of school for a term and going to Europe. And so, we had a great few weeks spending time together, reading, learning, and doing maths – her favourite! I was petrified in the beginning; what if I stuffed up her entire education? But on the second day she sat and read a book for two hours and I had never seen her read for more than two minutes prior – so that gave me the confidence that we were on the right path. And just like Pencils we are both learning as we are going. What I love is that Oli thinks having a charity in your house is what everyone does so I love that she feels that helping others and being a humanitarian is something that we should all be involved in.

We are continuing our alternative education this year for Olive because it works well for her, and it works well for Pencils, especially if we have to go away or do presentations. It makes me think of education as a whole, what it actually is and why school works for some and not for others. We love a morning on the beach studying marine life or doing science experiments at home…and maths is still her favourite.

I actually adore getting to spend this extra time with my daughter. We have more time to discuss things that are going on in her world and also the wider world. We get more time to go on walks, have adventures and we have none of the troubles that plagued us at school. It feels a little selfish on my part, but I think when I look back I will be so grateful I could do this for us both.

It's about finding *more life in the hours* rather than *finding more hours in the life*. Something that is a new mantra for me this year. And I know, when I ask Olive regularly, would she like to go back to school, she replies, 'No way Mum, I love home-school, can we start early today?' And I guess…that was the type of answer I was looking for all along.

I am grateful that I live in a country where I have these options and choices to make. If I need some new resources I can go to the library, Google it, download it, or pop into Officeworks and buy it. In many countries where we send pencils, that choice isn't available and in other countries they are so poor that they try to home-school, but many have not been taught reading or writing so getting around, reading signs, and home-schooling is not an option. And so, the cycle of challenging and reduced education persists. Many of the children stay working on the family farm or family business. None of it is easy for them.

Val is another amazing friend; she has spoken to me so much about energy. About allowing good energy in and letting bad energy out. She is my guide and protector (as she often laughs) as I say 'yes' to everything and then she asks me to question it and prioritise it. She's always right and I love her for being protective of me also. I am her Padawan.

Here are some special words from Val Sardon – 2IC (Pencils Community & Operations and Logistics Legend!)

What's the excitement of a PENCIL?

I wondered!

Yes, there are lead ones, coloured ones, short ones, and long ones. So?

Now I get it! It's what they do and where they go!

Little did I know that when I met Cindy some couple of years ago that I would have this new and exciting direction with a Pencil.

I recall one morning scanning through the Facebook pages as we do and noticed a call Cindy put out for pencil cases. I thought that since I don't physically have the time to volunteer at this point I could very easily drive down to Officeworks, buy a few cheap ones and donate them. Once there I spotted a range of strong but cheap cases on the bottom shelf, so I loaded up with about twenty.

As I was struggling to stand upright I became aware of a loud conversation between a mum and daughter and then had the realisation that mum couldn't afford what the daughter wanted. I could feel their frustration and see their frustration. I felt the look they were giving me. Here I am standing with all this stock in my arms and they are arguing over something so much less.

The feeling and that look went straight to my heart!

I quickly picked up a few more items like pencils, rubber, ruler etc. and asked the woman who was now trying to calm after her rage, to wait there for a moment and I would be back. I quickly made my way to the cash register, paid for all my selection and promptly went back to this woman and her daughter who were still waiting as I had asked.

I had also asked the salesperson to put a selection of items in a separate bag which I lovingly and proudly handed to this woman saying, 'here is my gift to you, please give it to your daughter and enjoy the day!' She looked stunned as she glanced towards her daughter and handed it over. I smiled, turned as I made my move towards my car and on with the rest of the day with my heart smiling. Something so simple gave me so much joy.

I have reflected on this incident many times and thought, charity begins at home and there are simple needs all around us, we just need to become more aware.

With this new awareness I then took more notice of what Cindy was up to when she put out a call for volunteers for a couple of hours to sort out Pencils.

I thought to myself 'here we go again... it's the Pencil,'

Within Cindy's home on the ground floor is a room that I am sure was designed to be a casual lounge area but no, it's loaded full of boxes and boxes of Pencils and all sorts of accessories that go with a Pencil.

At this point I confess to having a background in decluttering and have experience where I have assisted many to declutter their spaces. On looking at Cindy's room of boxes I looked and thought I need to put my hand up and assist. I need to draw on all my skills here! There was no judgement but rather, the pencils really were creating a Community and a life of their own at their own escalating speed, we needed to try and structure a bit more flow for the ease of all.

On sharing my thoughts with Cindy, we created a plan and as the pencils and all their accessories continue to flow in, we have to keep reconstructing the plan of flow. This flow has now moved beyond the walls of the lounge room into an adjoining room and then Lynn, one of the volunteers, was able to donate an outdoor metal shed which is filling quickly. Oh, the life of a Pencil.

This last week Cindy and I thought it was time to introduce ourselves to Bunnings with the thought of 'shelving' in our minds. Might they have some old shelving they no longer have a need for, might they hear our story and wish to donate, might they offer a discount if we purchase? Being a new and growing Community based on volunteers, we had no money!

In no time at all we were introduced to Rob who was absolutely delightful and helpful. We believe that we are now in line for a donation of shelving. Thank you, Bunnings, our new favourite place!

More streamlining, all in a pursuit of being able to access items quickly and easily when a call for help comes in. Our aim is to be able to expedite requests for help quickly and simply.

On reflection, I see the power of the Pencil!

With a Pencil, we can write and draw.

In collecting so many Pencils, we need volunteers to sort and sift.

A collection of volunteers to sort a collection of Pencils means meeting new and amazing people and make new friends.

All these boxes and boxes of Pencils stay out of landfill and become a source of joy to kids who have little or none, anywhere in the world. Oh, the joy of a Pencil.

With so much love and support for me as a person, it is easy to make steps and decisions about the direction of Pencils Community. I have gained a lot of insight and perspective into who I am and what I want Pencils to be. It's been years of growth to get here and I hope moulded by my friendships and mentors I have mentioned. I have also gained the insight and support of so many wonderful people through the years. Trines, Cath, Ange, Dan, Shane, Kaz, Kat, John, and Gail deserve a very special mention here. They are all near and dear to my heart, have shared their wisdom and advice and support for me. They have helped me to put my best foot forward and had my back throughout all the tough times in life and laughed with me through all the wonderful times - I am so grateful for them all!

People often wonder what the true life of a humanitarian is – hopefully you see, that for me, life is still pretty regular and normal – well to us it is. We have certainly had people say to us over the last few years that our life is anything other than normal. We like to think it is though – these are the choices that we have made for ourselves and each other to be happy and it is living in this pure and authentic way that has led us to where we are now – growing and learning daily, perhaps in just a less traditional way to some but what seems perfectly clear to us.

Hi Cindy, I heard you on the radio last week and I just had to message you. I don't normally do these sort of things... but your story really touched. I have Lyme's disease and your positive outlook on life is refreshing and inspiring to me. Thank you from the bottom of my heart.

Kel xoxo

CHAPTER 13

Warts and All: The 'Other' Real Truth Behind Being a Humanitarian

If you have read up to here and are intrigued about becoming a humanitarian, about living the life and road less travelled filled with purpose and passion, I have something to tell you. If you have read these beautiful stories about real humans achieving greatness, then I must be 100% honest with you. I need to tell you everything, so you have the full gamut of information. This is not to deter you but to keep it real – this is your backstage pass remember, your behind-the-scenes look, warts and all, to become that Humanitarian Rockstar!

Just as there is as much focus on finding your purpose and getting involved in humanitarian efforts, there is also the strong likelihood of burnout at some stage.

Humanitarian work can go one of two ways – it can empower you and charge you up – or it can drain the very life out of you. I have seen both in the charity sector and a lot of it comes down to balance and self-care as well as 'exposure on the ground'.

Do you remember back in the 70s and 80s when rockstars would drink and get high with white powdered substances before taking the stage? They would smash up guitars and hotel rooms, it would be a drug-fuelled anarchy all in the name of finding that sweet tune. Most of it would be in anticipation before the concert, then after the massive high would come the crashing and depressive lows.

However, these days you are more likely to find that the sex, drugs and rock 'n' roll have been replaced and traded for high-tech, wellbeing, and professionalism. Many a rockstar now tours with personal chefs in order to stay healthy for their long tours on the road; they can be devoted to meditation and many are yogis and prefer to use their smartphones to stay connected to family and their many devoted fans.

They are more likely to be connected internally within themselves rather than looking for external gratification. Although we still do have some hard-core rockers around that still fit the old bill, so you can be safe to assume that rock 'n' roll is not dead at all.

For anyone who has been involved in charity work knows that it quickly becomes your whole world. In fact, your entire universe. You work more hours, spend more time planning your charity or project when you are not working; your colleagues or project members become your comrades rather than your team and you begin to become isolated from your 'other' world as you know it.

For a while you have one foot in either camp; you can talk of your charity work and you can still talk about a movie you saw last week or the new handbag that you 'just had to have'. But over time you begin to examine your spending habits and value or worth in this sector and you begin to find idle conversation about movies or the weather just unrelatable.

This is especially true for those that have been on the ground, with poverty and trauma staring at you in the face. It's hard to justify the money for a handbag when you now can see how that money would help save a child's life of hunger or put them through schooling. You start to feel gluttonous! And then guilty. You have now crossed the threshold, and it's safe to say that not many humanitarians can return back. Ever.

The addictive nature of humanitarian work can lead you to come back for more and more each time. Lured by just one more project, one more orphanage to visit, one more water sanitisation unit to be installed or one more child that you can help. It can ensure that you have a feeling of being 'needed' for a greater purpose in life, that YOU are making a difference in this world, that you matter and have value.... and this makes you have a strong sense of self.

It is generally around about this time that you have begun to identify your sense of purpose, unless you have already previously got there. These humanitarians feel empowered and charged up by their new world. They are ignited by their purpose, they are passionate about their purpose, and they have endless energy to pursue their dream. They have no excuses.

Then there are those that have been in the game for a while. They have seen things, learnt things, things that they may want to un-see, but can't. They may see that the issue is bigger than what they first thought, that it starts to become overwhelming. So many children, so much trauma.

It's not surprising then that many humanitarians can suffer from burnout at some point along the way. Sometimes it begins as physical with the exposure to reduced sleep, skipping meals, or circumstances such as where you are staying on the ground, reduced accommodation standards, reduced medications, or simply that you may be getting sick, malaria and other things often happen on location.

Then there is the emotional side, the stories that stay with you, the faces that haunt you – there is no time to go and have wine in the hot springs now when you can't escape the images firmly implanted within your own mind. Sometimes the burnout causes problems re-entering back into society and some try desperately to leave all together. The very same humanitarians who were once desperate to get involved, now on the flip side.

Burnout can be more common than what you think and the value of self-care is extremely important and delicate at this time. In fact, critical at this time with the levels and situations being exposed to sometimes creating a post-traumatic stress situation. This overload can begin to create scenarios around their levels of expectation. Did they know what they were getting themselves into? Could they know? If they did know would they have still wanted to help or become a humanitarian? This in turn creates confusion around what their purpose is – did they not find it? Or do they simply need to take a recharge to come back stronger than ever. In fact, is that not what every rockstar does? Has their meltdown, shaves their head, and then comes back for the greatest 'comeback show' ever!

The very small percentage of people that leave this sector altogether have faced a metamorphosis of ginormous proportions. They often feel ostracised for 'leaving the cause', isolated because their comrades lack the understanding of why the person is leaving in the first place. Some face the real possibility of, where do I even live now? Where is my home now? Some may have become so transient and lived location to location out of a backpack, that they are unsure as to where they live or even where they belong.

Re-entry into 'civilian' life after a humanitarian mission can also lead one to question why they are back and are they better off living in the extreme conditions. In many cases it can become PTSD as the internal struggle rages on. Many miss the adrenaline of humanitarian projects, the endorphins from feeling so great about helping people within a community.

Many struggle to return to the more traditional life of materialistic items and many find themselves returning to the charity sector at some point again, perhaps just in a different capacity. Because the hardest part about leaving this sector is that it once held all the answers to your questions. Why I am here? Can I really make a difference in this world? When you chose to leave, you are choosing to leave that part of yourself. Suddenly, you are left with having to realign your goals, set new boundaries for yourself, your morals and passionate nature is called into question, what is your sense of 'self' now? And ultimately, the biggest and most confusing question of all, which now fills you with paralysis is…what is my purpose now?

Is it still the same, are you just exhausted and have burnout? Are you suffering from PTSD or was this not your true purpose all along? Suffering burnout in the early stages of setting up a charity is particularly fraught with dangers for failure because at this point in the journey you are 'bootstrapping' your way through. This means that you are doing and managing most of the tasks yourself. If you fall apart in this phase before you have systems in place or before you have contingency plans in place, then you are more likely to fail now than ever. If you fall over now, so does the whole thing!

I know from my experience that if you come unstuck in this phase it is very difficult to stay on course. The key for Pencils has been to build such an amazing team of people coming to us with the right intentions that it has been able to continue even at times due to my lack of great health. Many a job or project has been managed from the sidelines by me on crutches.

For the humanitarians that do fall off the wagon, so to speak, it doesn't have to spell the end. You can't just treat the symptom without addressing the cause. The key is to learn from the burnout experience. To learn that self-care and balance are a necessary and essential part to pace themselves throughout projects. They learn to take care of themselves, so that they can maintain the endurance race and not the sprint. It is the marathon of life, humanitarian work! But it sometimes requires rest and time away.

And like many a rockstar now with their tech and fine-tuning they are often able to make a choice about coming back into the sector. They may come in to the charity in a different capacity that may suit their life choices better. They may have a relationship or children and want to spend more time with them, than abroad. Or for some, they pack up their family with them each time and experience it all together.

Because being a humanitarian can come in many ways – balanced ways. Just because you might be the 'white women in the kitchen shelling peas and saving the world' doesn't make your role any less valuable than the person out in the field. Nor does the child that gets up at her school assembly and bravely talks about how they can all help as a school. Is her role any less than the person taking the suitcase full of educational items to the other side of the world? No.

What it comes down to is how authentic your purpose is to you – to your heart. If the key is balance and authenticity then they can actually get the life they want, not the one they think you should have.

Your life's experiences will help you find your true purpose if you let it and listen to what your heart and soul are telling you. That is what being authentic to yourself is all about. And once you have found that, your purpose follows. And once you've found that, you my friend, are the Rockstar that has the greatest comeback album of all time – because this time you are a Humanitarian Rockstar that knows how to maintain and run your endurance race with style and determination. Your inner fire is lit!

Big questions and decisions, right? Told you I would tell you the real behind-the-scenes look. Warts and all.

When we were kids, Mum would take our used stationery with her whenever she visited family in the Philippines. She would distribute, pencils, books, clothes, and non-perishable food. These are basic items which we often take for granted. We lost mum a few years ago and when I heard about Pencils Community I couldn't wait to get in touch and offer help in some way! Cindy has created a beautiful, far reaching project that opens up a world of opportunities for children less fortunate. She works tirelessly for others and I am honoured to be part of the wonderful community she has built.

Lynn Liu V.

CHAPTER 14

Developing an Attitude for Gratitude

That's an odd title for a chapter isn't it? Why gratitude, what is that about? If you are going to be a humanitarian, I've spoken previously about trusting your gut and bootstrapping. Having the confidence in yourself to do the things that feel 'right'. Yet this has a flipside. The courage to know that you can **always** learn more. About yourself, about your industry and be grateful for the lessons you can learn along the way. I have often said that being sick has been my greatest teacher, my 'mountain', which I must learn to climb through its sharp passages to its green pastures.

Part of this is to maintain a self-questioning nature. Can I do this better? Can I learn from this? There are two main questions that run through my mind constantly, they are:

1. What am I learning about myself? (Know thy Self)
2. What makes me think I have what it takes to run a charity in this wider world filled with humanitarian issues. (Know thy Ledge)

Know thy Self

To me, the definition of self-love, is when you can truly look yourself in the mirror and say, 'Hey, I am doing ok – I have my good bits and flaws but on the whole, I am happy being me.' They say that the people who have lost the most are the ones that have the most to give – because they know what it feels like, and the desire for no one else to have to experience what they have, is extremely powerful.

Like many, I am my harshest critic, and any judgement that someone else may have of me does not compare to my own self-criticism. So, to self-accept means I must welcome all the parts that make up me and understand them.

Some parts I welcome more than others, but I know ultimately, I must welcome them all and that at any point I can turn and look in the mirror and begin work on the aspects that, well, need some extra.

I often get called Wonder Woman or more by friends and get told by colleagues that I shouldn't be so humble about the work we achieve at Pencils Community. It's not something I am comfortable with, but I am getting better at it. Somewhere on the scale of selfless and selfish I need to end up somewhere in the middle.

I'm not quite there yet even though what we achieve is beyond my wildest imagination. Self-belief and self-love comes from many places and I believe gets easier with age. There are many out there who still struggle with a self-love concept – but all I can say is that we keep on keeping on. As I saw my message reflected back through Dion's eyes on stage that day, then and only then, did I really start to think about what I and our team had built and created.

So, here's what I know and some handy hot tips for knowing thy self:

- Know who you are – and if you don't – start learning! And never stop!
- Live – everyday!

- Everyone should at some point consider their expiry date! I have had to consider this and face my demons and think of my WHY am I here on this earth. I have thought about what legacy I want to leave, so that my daughter knows who I was. WHY? In thinking about death (morbid I know) I have actually liberated myself to live, every day.
- Don't wear masks, be authentic, live a true life full of purpose and change. I recently read and love the saying, '*You die a little every day. Actually, that is bullshit! You live every day of your life and die only on one day*'.
- '*You should leave this world in a better way than when you came into it*' said Scott Rosicka's Grandmother. You don't get much better advice than that.
- No excuses.
- Let go of the ones holding you back from what you wish to achieve.
- Even when you can't see or are lost, if you open your heart and mind you will see everything you need.
- Go camping! It does wonders for the soul.
- Try and keep some magic in your heart for as long as possible, like forever!
- If you have regrets – learn from them.
- Reset your brain to tell YOU the things that you know you want to be.
- Develop an attitude…for gratitude.

Know thy Ledge:

I read an interesting study recently about the 'happiest man in the world'. Happiness is something that everyone wants, right? And yet it evades most of us – unless we make a choice. So what choice did the happiest man in the world make? It is about how he looks at the world.

The study looked at **Matthieu Ricard,** a Frenchman who became a Buddhist monk and examined his brain function in response to certain stimuli. When shown a picture of something dark, say for example the devastation around an earthquake or tidal wave, Matthieu, expressed *compassion,* but did not internalise.

In every modern tragedy, like terrorist acts, they say look for the hero in that moment. When people have been mowed down in trucks by terrorists, they say don't look at the whole picture; it's too overwhelming and shocking! They say look for the person saving the child on the street otherwise you would just be in disbelief. They are the heroes and stories of joy in the dark moments. They become the light within the dark.

A friend of mine, Jase, and I were having a discussion and he showed me a picture of darkness from the day's events. I was shocked and devastated of an image of an injured child, in a war-torn country. The child was numb from the events that had befallen him. I felt it on a deeply personal level. As a mother I related to seeing a child in pain and wanting to help, and knowing I couldn't, hurt me.

Jase told me to flip it around and look for the opportunity to help and bring light. It's the same message as above. However, it is a new way for me to look at things. A new life lesson!

Know thy ledge, and here are my top tips.

- Don't freeze – do something. Anything. (I remember when my friend Jaime Ramos (SANCSS) was telling me about some kids in the Philippines living next to the waste dump – effectively, the 'tip' and also their main food source. With worms coming out their mouths from eating food in the dump, their ragged clothes, no shoes, dirty, and sick. I can imagine their faces, and it's heart breaking. It can become all-consuming, overwhelming, the stuff of nightmares if you let it – and so you have to stop and focus on what you can do. If I thought about the entire scenario of poverty, I may be compelled to freeze and do nothing

- I just wouldn't know where to start! It's too big! So, I have to believe that our Pencil packs for these beautiful children are the closest thing that I can do to replicate to some kind of magic and something special for them, but mostly I want them to experience and not give up on hope.
- Understand your environment.
- Learn different points of view, from as many people and places that you can…then figure yours out.
- Be happier – choose it:

There's an apparent paradox in modern life: Society as a whole is getting smarter, yet we aren't any closer to figuring out how to all get along. 'How is it possible that we have just as many, if not more, conflicts as before?' asks social psychologist Igor Grossmann at the University of Waterloo in Canada. Studies have found that people who live in poorer communities are happier and wiser. As a community they have learnt to compromise, have better conflict resolution, negotiate better and live with one another as opposed to the middle and upper class who outsource a lot and essentially become increasingly isolated. They lose their tribe and village as they get further up the economic ladder.

(Author: Eranda Jayawickreme;
Reference Article: 'The lower your social class
the wiser you are', Michael Price, 2017)

- It can be simple and make sense (look at Pencils – it's not rocket science, it just makes sense and the concept is really easy to understand.)
- Find your true path and stick to it.
- Ask yourself the burning question, what's holding you back? What ledge is in your way or what ledge are you sitting on? What are you waiting for? Ask yourself.

- Now that you know your ledges, fears and obstacles, break them down further to see if you can overcome them and identify your true path and purpose.

I have my purpose and I know WHY…I do what I do.

I know WHAT I do, but how many of us really know WHY we do something? This is a question that I always had in me, and so too did I have the answer, but it took time and the model of Pencils to give me a way to find it and have clarity.

What's my WHY you ask? It's simple:

It's saving lives and changing lives by giving hope and opportunity to those in need. It's about connecting with all humans, especially children to create a village, a community, a Pencils Community.

'But it's just a flippin' pencil?' you ask.

But a pencil can make a huge difference. It is a tool that can change lives, empower children, and propel hope, opportunity and an education so that they too can create change. Change within themselves, their lives, their future.

That is why our motto is 'helping children colour their world'. It is about every unique child's story that we can help and change. It isn't just a percentage of people living in poverty; these children are more than just a statistic. They are, all of our children, each with their own background and life story and experiences, some traumatic but it is THEIR story.

I want to be able to provide them with a little magic and a lot of hope. This is my WHY and it is the most powerful question you can ever ask yourself and find the answer too.

For those that live in a space and complain, whinge and moan as if on autopilot… for those that can get caught up in the complaining (*as we all can at times), I urge you to keep coming back to the question:

Why should the world dedicate itself to making you happy? What are you bringing back to the world?

There is a common saying that many of us use; we throw our hands in the air, we look to the horizon and find ourselves saying, 'it's up to the universe'. We look outside to find the answers. And while doing all these things bring profound peace, sunsets, starry nights, and others, it is the inner universe we must honour.

That is the key to finding happiness and your purpose.

You have to ignite your own spark, light your own candle, before you can pass it on to the future generations. (This isn't the same as passing on a family business to your children, it's about passing on the happiness and purpose, the essence of who you are to others.)

Because in the end, we are all looking for the same thing, higher purpose and connection (even though our purpose might be different) we still desire our own internal divine.

Great to hear you so positive no matter what happens with the disease always remember what a superstar you are and that you are so much stronger than anything that does to you. Thank you, superstar! You inspire me to work harder for others in need through all your challenges that you face! Can't wait to catch up!

Michael G.

CHAPTER 15

Ambassadors - Here We Grow!

What makes someone want to give back? To become inspired to volunteer? To take significant time out of their day and give it to the service of others? It's a question with many varied and compelling responses. In my role as Founder and CEO, I come across volunteers all the time, and their reasons for volunteering fascinate me. What I find even more intriguing is the people who then go on to take a larger volunteer role in an organisation – for us, that means becoming a 'Pencils Ambassador'.

What does being a Pencils Ambassador mean? Our definition is someone willing to be a 'drop-off' point for Pencils and collect items on our behalf. Generally, they have to have the space and the desire to be inundated with boxes! We then set up plans with each Ambassador to move the pencils along.

Most of our Ambassadors are regional or located in other states and cities. The idea being that the pencils are collected and dropped off and then our pencil recipients tend to be more local. For instance, we have Ambassadors in Perth who are working with organisations to move the pencils direct into regional and remote parts of Western Australia. So, an Ambassador is willing to go the extra mile and support local projects and lead the way (with our support of course).

The most common reason we have people wanting to help Pencils Community in a broader role as an Ambassador is because they have a personal experience that connects them to the cause. To me this is the most empowering of all the reasons to help because the individual has a deep personal connection. It could be the mind-set of, 'that could have been me as a child', if they have witnessed trauma or abandonment. It could be they have witnessed children in need on their travels, or they may want to make a direct difference in the field of education.

Yet believing that they can now make a difference in the life of someone else is the key. Belief, hope, opportunity they can now create for another. And in doing so, they help themselves too.

Volunteering also has a great impact on the individual – from making one feel good about themselves, releasing tension, lowering stress levels, connecting with other like-minded individuals and helping to give greater awareness and perspective of their own lives in the context of the wider world. It is a powerful psychology to be 'doing good' for one's own value in the community.

And other less common responses are that it looks good on the resume or is good for business and clients, or it helps students get into school scholarship programs and teaches them news skills. All of these responses still exist and are valid for the individual too.

There has also never been an easier time to 'do good' in the world. There is a plethora of charities in which to volunteer. What makes Pencils Community unique is that it is also easy for the kids to get involved, thereby starting the conversation early about others that are less fortunate and what we can do to help.

My good friend Gaynor brought her teenage daughter and a friend around for several weeks in a row. It gave them a great chance to see what it is like actually doing the practical work and making a difference. The one piece of feedback that I regularly get back is that you can 'actually' see the difference that pencils make to one individual – and so you feel the motivation and energy to keep going.

Pencils Community sets up a place for sharing with others and also a place for healing. I know by being up front and transparent about my illness and living with chronic pain that others start to open up about themselves and what is going on in their life. There are no masks in the Pencils room and it gives peoples a chance to begin to get to know each other and let their guard down. We also have a lot of fun and there are always a lot of laughs, banter, and bonding going on in the Pencils room.

What started out as a Melbourne-based hobby has sprawled across the country with the same model being replicated on some level throughout Australia and New Zealand. We have many new Ambassadors signing up daily – it is amazing the love that Pencils can bring.

But from the day we began we have had a few main Ambassadors on board. To them I especially say thank you and express my gratitude. They offered to collect pencils on behalf of me and Pencils Community before any strategies or processes were in place. They just had a strong belief in the cause, it made sense, and they had faith in us all along. Now we are finding projects and moving the items on to worthwhile destinations, but like everything worth waiting for, it all takes time to grow organically and develop.

Western Australia - *Perth and Busselton*

Kristy came on board as one of my very first Ambassadors. As a teacher she knew first-hand what a difference education can make to the lives of an individual. I remember laughing with her about sorting pencils as we watched our favourite reality show at the time. I avoided the spoiler in the finale as Perth was two hours behind Melbourne.

As time went on we exchanged more on a personal level and became friends. This is the case with all Ambassadors, as you get to know them more through their work and their pursuit to do good.

145

Kristy has often said to me, 'the healing and soothing space that comes with sorting pencils is magic. And so importantly is that 'connectedness'…we all have our 'stories' we all have things that break our hearts…and we all have things that put us back together again.'

I remember vividly Kristy telling me of her son, Cohen, who suddenly lost a friend of his to a brain aneurysm. The friend, just eleven years old. She explained to Cohen that you must simply make every day count, because you never know. She went on to tell me what a huge wake-up call it was for her, that she had practised gratitude and kindness, but this took it to a whole new level. Watching her son grieve for his friend was one of the hardest things a mother can stand by (helplessly) and watch.

Kristy used to say to me that some days they just sat there and sorted pencils. It was Kristy's way of being present with her son without him having to talk. I know that Pencils had also helped Kristy at a time when her career hadn't worked out the way she thought it would.

'I hadn't realised how disconnected I had become from spending years as a full time working mum... disconnected from my son... community... where I was working was tough... loved the kids... but when you let go of what's not meant for you... the right things start to come in... sorting those pencils got me through one tough time.'

Since then Kristy and I have swapped events in our lives and shared thoughts and feelings. It is so lovely knowing someone like Kristy and it is gorgeous to watch her and her son grow and go from strength to strength. She now has a teaching position she loves, and her son has just begun secondary school. Life moves on and it is a privilege to be a part of their lives. One day we will meet – but I love for now that Pencils brought us together and helped foster a gorgeous friendship.

Next to join the WA contingent was Mandy. Mandy was a parent at a school and showed huge initiative in getting a pencils collection started.

Since then I have connected Mandy and Kristy together – although only a few hours apart I know that we will connect as a group and make great projects happen from their collections in WA. Mandy comes up with some amazing ideas and it is so exciting to have her refreshing energy around.

'I stumbled upon Pencils Community while searching online one day and was drawn to it…I needed to find out more. After looking at the Facebook Page and reading about all the amazing work Cindy and the rest of the Pencils Community had been doing, I wanted to be a part of this wonderful project,' said Mandy.

'I contacted Cindy immediately. Her story about how Pencils came about – 'while cleaning out her daughter's desk and she couldn't bring herself to throw out her old pencils', resonated with me. I went through the same dilemma at the start of every school year, when a new packet of pencils was purchased as part of the book list. Although I would usually donate the old pencils to a local Op Shop. I love, now that I am a part of Pencils Community, knowing that my pencils and those that have been kindly donated by others, go directly to those who really need them, both here at home and overseas.

'I feel so privileged to be a part of Pencils Community, to be able to help those who are less fortunate, to be able to make their future brighter and as the Pencils mission statement says, 'help children to colour their world'.'

Tasmania – *Burnie & Launceston*

At the end of 2016, a lovely teacher by the name of Bec Van Est first got in touch with us to enquire about how she could get her pencils collection to us in Melbourne. At this time, we had no Ambassadors in place, nor anyone we knew close to her in Launceston, so she decided to fundraise at her school to have them sent over by courier on the ship that goes between Tassie and Melbourne.

Bec organised a bake sale at her school and called it 'Slice Slice Baby'. All of the teaching staff got involved and not only did they raise enough money to send over the pencils to Pencils HQs in Melbourne, (which I was lucky enough to greet in my PJs one morning at 7am), but Bec kindly sent over the remaining money to go towards projects that we were doing at Pencils Community. We started to really understand the connections that we were developing within our communities, with the teachers and the children – who we later got to visit with our good friend Sarah (Lion Heart) later that year.

A month after learning of Bec and the great pencil collection going on in Launceston, another lovely teacher by the name of Nicole Chettle got in touch with me in September 2016. The one detail that I forgot to ask was where is she based, assuming that travel and distance in Tasmania would be close. Launceston and Burnie are over 100 kms apart. Now when I say lessons were learnt the hard way in the beginning, this is one of the lessons I meant.

But lessons are a place for learning and from this simple omission and a clear demand in Tasmania, we established an Ambassador in Ulverstone (Tasmania). It just so happened that my good friend, Micheline Andrews lived in Tasmania and when she learnt of our mayhem she offered to become our first Tasmanian Ambassador. And it would turn out to be the most wonderful blessing in disguise.

Micheline and Nicole were pivotal in spreading the love of Pencils, speaking at a women's networking lunch and the local Lions Club dinner. From here we gained, Melissa Bell and Sarah Bosch and also Melissa's sister, Alex Bell. This group would form an even bigger project in 2017 called Project: Lion Heart in which we would all come together as a unified team, with myself and family travelling over to Tasmania on a huge roadshow.

Following this event, we also picked up Frank McKechnie as a Pencils Ambassador. Frank, an Army veteran, is a great asset to our

Tassie team and a firm supporter in our programs to help returned veterans.

New South Wales - *Sydney*

Like all good things at Pencils Community, Maggie was referred to us through a friend of ours, Jasmin. We had a need for an Ambassador in NSW and just like that she appeared. Sometimes people are sent to us for a reason, and I waited until our connection arose.

At this point Maggie was based in Sydney and one of our newest Ambassadors, coming on board at the end 2017, just in time for the end of the school year, one of our busiest times. She did everything she was supposed to as an Ambassador and then one day got in touch with a minor problem for us to solve. She had been giving me breathing space as she knew that December is extremely busy, and I was also unwell over this period. It was through our communication that we connected and realised our values aligned.

Maggie shared with me that she was a single mother who had raised and educated seven children – all of whom are working and leading productive lives. And with a growing tribe of grandchildren too! She is a cancer survivor (no recurrence in ten years) after two consecutive battles within six months. Resilience and strength are the words that come to mind.

She had recently lost her own beloved mother and best friend two years ago and it was an incredible loss to her. Her mother was eighty-nine and had survived five different kinds of cancer to fall, hit her head and then suddenly she was gone. Grief has taught her the urgency to value every moment and not to squander even a second because we don't know how much time we all have left. Something that resonates with me strongly. It has become a part of her that she has learnt to navigate. She knows what it feels like to just breathe, figure out what to do next and then take one step and breathe again. 'They all add up,' she reassures me. She has belief and hope and she is a true survivor!

I could relate to everything that Maggie was saying because I have experienced my own form of loss. For myself. My health being the primary target; feeling like things were being taken away from me, like time and experiences I couldn't physically do anymore. I felt robbed of life and betrayed by my own body for not working better, not working the way I wanted it too! Watching my hand as it tried to pour sugar into my coffee, knowing my brain was telling it to do so but my nerves saying, let's drop it on the floor instead. But, then I learnt to stop and breathe. To figure it out and then step forward, navigating in a new way – learning to live with my 'new kind of normal'. Besides, less sugar in my coffee is better for me anyway.

I learnt to be grateful for my body for working so hard to be well, loving it instead of hating it for letting me down. I learnt to be grateful that I had coffee and electricity to boil the water, that I had a roof over my head and skills that I could use, like for Pencils. I could be awake late into the night creating, just to need that coffee in the first place in the morning. Life has a way of bringing people into it when you need them most. And I am so grateful I have been able to meet Maggie and learn from her and be able to relate to her.

Maggie spends her time healing as an accomplished artist and creative and understands the importance and relationship of having tools to draw, colour, and create with – just like our kids. She is getting ready to enter one of the most prestigious art competitions of all time. She is a perfect addition to the Pencils Ambassador team. She is our Saint Pollyanna of Perpetual Hope!

South Australia - *Adelaide*

Our South Australian Ambassador is in the pipelines! She is nearly up and ready to take deliveries and come on board but has had a busy start to the year like many school mums! Soon we will have updates for our South Australian neighbours.

Victoria – *Melbourne and Regional Centres*

Our Victorian team really comes from a combination of volunteers who became Ambassadors by accident. Kaz and Kat have been on board since day one! Kaz as you know has helped with so many facets of Pencils and it was Kat who was our first Ambassador to visit an orphanage in Bali and the second country we ever visited for Pencils Community. Months later Angela (or as we affectionately call her, Big-Hair Angela) also visited an orphanage in Bali and distributed items to the children in need. These beautiful friends have helped at many a pencil-sorting day. Also to visit Bali was my great friend Michelle (Sally) who paid extra for overweight luggage herself (due to the huge amount of pencils she packed) just to make sure the pencils arrived safely. So generous!

Of course, Pencils couldn't exist without our Victorian Ambassadors who drive the 'mother ship'. Lynne, Gaynor, Phyllis, Sheena, Ange, Jo, Lynn, Jules, and of course Val deserve a special mention here. As do Jaime Ramos (SANCSS), Michael Gallus (Footys4All) and Bela Mitchell (OrphFund) / Mel McGaw (OrphFund) also. As do my Mum and her brother-in-law Gary (and my Aunty Cheryl) who regularly donate pencils weekly to my house!

Jo Howard, new to Team Pencils, has come on board and saved my administration efforts. She is a dynamite and has helped me to get on top of the now thousands of emails and messages I receive. Rather than get overwhelmed with the sheer volume, which I must say is easily done, Jo has been able to come in and help take control and organise. I am so grateful for her help and I am learning more about delegating to others and letting people help because they want too. She is a great asset to Pencils and we are lucky to have her.

We have been lucky enough for our local schools to come on board to help in so many ways. From Pencils Collections to programs called 'Community Connections' which I taught at a local high school for six weeks. There at Patterson River Secondary College I met and worked with the incredible Janet Mitchell and Matt Clarke. Both champions of Pencils. I recall one day a chain of thirty teachers in my driveway acting as a human chain carrying in approximately three tonnes of text books in a production-like way, passing from one to another as a team! Amazing! Creating an ongoing relationship with them has been wonderful, talking to the Year Nine kids about humanitarian issues was an eye opener but in a great way. I learn so much from the kids every day. And it was Matt driving around with me in the car and trailer in December 2017 loading up pencils from each and every school who had donated. Friends for life. This got me thinking too about all the workplace stress that our teachers and School Principals are under and you know what happens when I get thinking…something new and massive will develop each time.

Queensland – *Gold Coast & Brisbane & Mount Isa*

In the middle of Mount Isa….my good friend Melissa North is on a mission. She is taking pencil supplies to the local Mount Isa hospital. She has been an Ambassador for well over a year and has helped co-ordinate pencils to arrive at a local community kindergarten as well as a drop-off for supplies that were taken to the border of the Northern Territory and Queensland to a remote Indigenous community. She has been pivotal as our western Queensland regional Pencils Ambassador and we are hoping to pay her a long overdue visit in 'the Isa' later this year bringing more pencils to the local children also.

'Lissie' as we call her, has been a friend of mine for a while. We met at the infamous Mt Isa seminar that Ocean and I presented at the Mt Isa Library. From the moment we met, we felt a deep connection to one another and became friends. We also had a lot in common as authors and made sure that after I had left the Isa we would keep in touch – we have been friends ever since. She is my gorgeous friend to talk to whenever I need, and she has been a supporter of all my endeavours as I have to hers.

It is so lovely to be a part of Pencils Community, with the amazing inspirational Cindy Rockstar. There is something wonderful and satisfying about helping kids colour their worlds and as a mother I feel it is great to give back to the community and raise awareness of this charity.

When I heard about Pencils, I just had to get involved. Words cannot express the look you see on the children's faces; how grateful they are to receive a gift of pencils. Who wouldn't feel great about doing something like that?

The thing I like most about Pencils is that I can fit it into my life around work and be part of creating projects. I can be as involved for as little or as much as I can spare the time. Knowing that all the time given, is going to help children somewhere in the world. as I have personally found out, even where I live in regional western QLD.

I also met a lovely person, Catherine Hopgood on my trip to Mt Isa. Both Catherine and her husband, David Hopgood (who is in the Army) helped support Pencils Community by assisting to get pencils from a business that was closing down, into a remote community school on the border of Queensland and the Northern Territory. It was amazing to think that our beloved pencils were now making their way into remote indigenous communities in Australia. Something that I had long hoped for.

Later, we were able to coordinate 60kg of art and craft supplies to five remote communities in Alice Springs with the help of Footys4All Founder, Michael Gallus. Michael generously offered us space in his courier delivery to Alice Springs and we were able to get a huge supply of much needed arts and crafts to over 200 indigenous children in the Northern Territory along with footballs, netballs, and soccer balls. We repeated this method with the assistance of Jaime Ramos (SANCSS) and the three of us together, coordinated another 60kg of pencils, stationery supplies and sporting goods to indigenous children in Croker Island, 200km north-east of Darwin, still part of Australia.

And in November 2017, I was lucky enough to be invited to speak at a Property Investment Conference in the Gold Coast. This was the beginning of the 'Corporates' coming on board. While this may sound like it had nothing to do with Pencils, it couldn't be further from the truth. 'Mike' or rather Mike Harvey (On Your Side Investments), whom I had met at the first Gold Coast event where I had my epiphany, had in fact caught up with me after that particular presentation.

He loved what he heard about Pencils Community and invited me to attend his presentation a few weeks later on the topic of 'purpose'. He told me that he would be travelling in India, Thailand, and Cambodia for some time but that he would book my flights and we would catch up. My parting words to him were, 'Hey, Mike – take some pencils with you overseas when you go.' and I flashed him a smile.

The phone rings, it's 8.30am. I've been up late the night before working until some random hour of 2am and so the morning is slow and the coffee not acting quick enough. 'It's Friday,' I think to myself, 'one more day of mayhem and then a weekend of different mayhem.' and I laugh at the busyness that my life has become.

'Hey, Cin, it's Mike, how are you?' comes the voice down the line. 'Don't suppose you've got some pencils around that I can take on my trip, do you?' he asks.

'Sure, I do, when do you go?' I enquire.

'I leave first thing Tuesday morning, like 4am.'

'I'll see what I can do!' and I excitedly get off the phone. I pull a hoodie on, put my hair into a ponytail and go straight to the post office. Now at this point, I know you know I am in my PJs, but to be fair they just kind of look like leggings at this stage, so I could almost be confused for being out early for a sporty run. But no, I am in the post office line, waiting to buy some express post bags to pack with pencils to see if I can get them to Mike in time from Melbourne to Queensland.

I estimate that about 8kg would be a good amount, assuming the weight baggage limit was between 20kg and 23kg. I rush home and pack the bags with pencils, colouring books, crayons, erasers, sharpeners, rulers, and stickers. I jump on and off the scales weighing the express bags each time. An hour later, I am back at the post office and sending them off – hoping they will be collected in the 10am morning collection. Well I must have had luck on my side because the items arrived, and Mike was thrilled.

Weeks pass and Mike's travels continue from city to city, from country to country, until he arrives in Thailand. On the day he decides to visit a local school and deliver the pencils and goodies, it is a national holiday. The children don't mind – they get dressed in their school uniform and line up for three hours waiting for what to them is 'royalty'. Mike sends me photos and messages that evening of his time at the school. The children's faces, how it made him feel. You can tell the experience moved him and brought him to tears. He told me that it was the highlight of his trip.

This was his introduction to me at the Property Investment Conference and I proceeded to talk to over one hundred people who have high-income or work with clients that do. I was there to speak on 'purpose' and as I told them my personal story I also explained to them why I felt I was the richest person in this room. Why? Because I knew my purpose in life, and to me and everyone else watching on who wanted to know their purpose, it was worth more than gold.

I relayed examples of volunteers, telling the story of how friends, John and Jeane, had taken the equivalent of their body weight over in pencils and flew into Hanoi (Vietnam). It had been arranged through a friend of a friend that our contact 'Jo' who lived in the small village in the South of Vietnam called, Mũi Né that she would assist.

The pencils were dropped off at a courier bus company office in Hanoi and couriered down south. At the same time a massive storm hit North Vietnam and our friends, John and Jeane could only make it as far south as Hội An. Stranded in the flood waters in a tiny hotel, their whole trip now a wipe-out, they decided to do what can only be described as amazing and selfless. They went out each day to a restaurant that was being used to pack food ration packs and they helped assemble four thousand ration packs for the stranded and displaced Vietnamese.

Now the pencils must have had luck on their side, because they made it all the way to Mũi Né and days later were taken to some local orphanages as intended. These children received goodies of pencils and stationery and specially handsewn pencil cases from our wonderfully giving friends, Roslyn and Alison. These two have (and still do) sew the most beautiful pencil cases and fill them up with goodies. Their most recent delivery containing magical tiny handsewn soft toys for the children.

Reine Clemow, from his company Acquira Wealth Partners walked right up to me after the Property Investment presentation and told me he was giving me a $500 donation for Pencils Community. I must have said something that connected with him and my audience then!

This reinforced my belief that we needed more Ambassadors around the country and it was on this trip that Ocean and Jason Smith (aka-Flash) agreed to be my Gold Coast and Brisbane Ambassadors, respectively. Three days after this property conference, an author handed pencils over to Ocean and in turn they were handed over to Dion; he left the Gold Coast with pencils packed and became our International Pencils Ambassador, being based in Singapore. Wow were we growing now!

International

On an international level we have the following magical Pencils Community Ambassadors in place with many new projects just beginning to 'kick- off' in these countries:

- Singapore – Dion (Pencils Community Ambassador and Lion Heart Ambassador)

- New Zealand – Marilyn & Amanda (Dion's Mum and Sister)
- Portugal – Rose Chandler
- We also have just had recent interest in the UK and USA also – STAY TUNED!

Junior Ambassadors

Part of our ethos at Pencils Community is being able to harness and empower the energy and hope of our Junior Ambassadors. We have come across many special children who have embraced the power of the pencil and created collections at their local school, conducted 'Pay it Forward' projects and created videos for us. Our good friend, Caroline has been advising us and helping with some future ideas here, exciting times!

We can only include a few of their contributions here but wanted to make special mention to Eva (who organised a huge Pencils package for Zambia and spent days and days over summer sorting and packing six hundred and fifty bundles of Pencils love). To Michaela for creating such a wonderful video for us with Flash! To Rihanna, Madeleine, and her amazing mum, Melissa Baker and family, as well as Isabelle (Pay it Forward Campaign) and her gorgeous mum, Jenny Mioni who coordinated a huge donation for us, made her own t-shirt and presented at her school to which we received our first huge regional Victorian donation. Even our country towns are now on board - we have become so well known!

A wonderful achievement from two inspiring teachers from Mentone Girls' Grammar School, Camilla Gaff, and Kylie Federici, who created a wonderful Junior Enterprise Group and steered the ship for students in Grades Two to Five. The aim was for students to understand a social enterprise, big business, charities, and more. Like a well-oiled machine these juniors could out-do most adults with their abilities, strategies, and processes and detailed business plans. Special mention to

Abigail and Ada, leaders of the Junior Enterprise Group from Mentone Girls' Grammar School who coordinated a massive collection of pencils for us.

Also to amazing Junior Ambassadors such as Maeve and Mason who continue to inspire us all. And to my gorgeous catering staff, my daughter Oli and her BFF Georgia for attending to the coffee making, drinks, and cookies for our volunteers.

And so many other wonderful Pencils Ambassadors who have really stepped up and sparkled.

Abigail's Story:
Project Manager, Social Enterprise
(Mentone Girls' Grammar School: Primary)

Over the last two terms, our Social Enterprise team has been working on a project for the Pencils Community.

Our goal was to receive as many donations of pencils and stationery as we could and have them all tested, sharpened and sorted for Cindy so that it would be easier and faster for her to get them sent off to children around Australia and the world.

Ada and I have project managed this together. We began by communicating our donation drive to our Junior School staff, students, and their families. We had to organise box drop-off points around our school so that people could easily donate and be reminded whenever they saw a Pencils Community box.

We worked through our lunchtimes to test every single item that had been donated. Most of our donations were in good working order, but some were ready for the bin!

Personally, I've been so inspired by Cindy's work with the Pencils Community. In the holidays, I worked with her at the Pencils Community headquarters to help sort pencils and stationery. Collecting the donations at school each week made me realise how hard it is to continuously do it.

One of the biggest challenges for our team was sorting through each week's new donations quickly but thoroughly. It is important that we worked together in groups and helped each other, even when there was a mountain of new donations.

In past projects, we each had our own special roles. This time, it was a bit different. We all had to work together as one big team to achieve the same goal. It actually made us all feel really connected as a group and we got to know each other a bit better as we sat together sharpening pencils and testing pens and textas!

The end result of our work kept us really motivated. We wanted to achieve a goal and push through the tough moments. We learnt a lot about perseverance because this project wasn't always sunshine and daisies, but we knew it was going to be worth it.

Ada Jenkins, Assistant Project Manager, Social Enterprise (Mentone Girls' Grammar School: Primary)

We are lucky children living in a lucky country. We've learnt that there are children around the world that are far less lucky than us. They deserve to have all that we have too. We have acted to help other children to have the things that we have and experience some of the fun that we have in our everyday lives.

I remember when Cindy told us about the time she delivered two grey lead pencils to a child who had very little. She told us how this child cried tears of happiness at receiving two pencils. I've remembered this story because Cindy's kindness caught my attention and it made me really want to help her and to help children.

Cindy told us about how her health has been affected by a bite from a tick. This makes her work much harder. Sharpening hundreds of pencils is a big task and it makes me proud to be helping her with her Pencils Community.

Our Junior Enterprise team has loved working with Cindy and her community and we would love to continue this partnership so that our small actions can make big change in our world.

Madeline's Story: (Mt Eliza Primary School)

'Just Like Me'

How it all started: There are so many poor countries in the world like Ghana, Malawi, Burundi, Bali, India, Uganda, and lots more. Australia is one of the wealthy countries and the kids here get lots of cool toys.

What I did: My brother and I had some old toys and stationery that we didn't use any more, so we gave it all to a place called the Pencils Community. In return the Pencils Community gave us some stuff because we were going to Bali soon.

When we were in Bali, we went to a poor village near Lovina. We gave the kids there some of our stuff and the stuff that the Pencils Community gave us. They were very happy, and it was good to see the smiles on their faces. I also went to a school where they could speak a little English. It was really cool.

Why I did it: I want to keep helping poor kids like the ones I saw and hopefully brighten up their day and put a smile on their faces. It's great to see kids who don't have what we have, so happy. I just think it's horrible that some people have to live like that and it shows that we are really really lucky.

How can you help? There are a few ways you can help but first I need to know if you're with me. Do you want to help poor kids who don't have what we have? Well, you can if you follow at least one of these suggestions:

- *At any time this year, if you have any spare stationery you can take it to the office and put it in the tub there.*
- *Ask your mum and dad to like the Pencils Community Facebook Page.*
- *Don't take your leftover stationery home at the end of this year because we will be collecting anything unwanted.*

Madeline also created some videos of her trying to speak Balinese as she handed out pencils also to the children. How beautiful and creative!

Mason's Story: (Pascoe Vale North Primary School)

On Saturday 20th January we took approximately thirty boxes filled with school supplies to Cindy Rochstein in Seaford who runs the Pencils Community charity.

As soon as we arrived, Cindy took seventy pencil cases to fill with pencils for a request for indigenous communities on Croker Island, which is 200km east of Darwin but still part of the Northern Territory.

Pencils Community has a big garage they use as storage and a sorting room! They have it full of boxes that have textas, pencils, and lots of other school supplies. They have volunteer sorting days where anyone, even kids, can go and help sort out the pencils and things. They have a box for each different colour of pencils and textas.

Some of our supplies will go to Croker Island, and Pencils Community also sends school supplies to orphanages and schools in the Philippines, Fiji, Africa, Vietnam, Nepal, New Zealand, and kids in Melbourne at the Les Twentyman Centre.

'By taking your discarded and used stationery Pencils Community can provide children with pencils, paper and pencil cases filled with goodies so that they too can embark on their education with the right tools. It gives them also an opportunity to create, learn, and develop; just as our kids do. We repackage and redistribute items to children in need, in orphanages and schools both in Australia and overseas so that every child receives pencils and an opportunity to 'colour their world'.'

Thank you to my friends, family, students, mums and dads, and teachers for all the donations at the end of last year. We also want people to know that anytime you are having a clean out (any time of the year) and have old school supplies you can give them to me or leave them at the office and we can pass them on to Pencils Community.

Mason Howard
5/6D
'Kids helping kids' ☺

Pencils Community, I would very much like to help with
packing and sorting etc.

Susan S.

CHAPTER 16

Nepal and a Lion

'Hi, my name is Sarah and I wanted to talk to someone about taking pencils over with me when I go to Nepal,' said a quiet voice on the other end of the line.

'Sure, great!' I say, 'When are you going?'

It's a late Saturday afternoon in May 2017. It's cool outside and I am getting ready to relax into the evening with a wine and some dinner.

'Monday,' comes the quiet reply. 'This Monday…' her voice trails off quietly.

Now I know I am good and resourceful at getting Pencils around the country, but I thought to myself, 'I'm not that good!'

But as is the 'Pencils way' where everything just falls into place at the exact moment it's meant to fall into place, I remembered that my good friend Micheline had been collecting pencils and had a great supply in her shed in Tasmania, and of course, was only a twenty-minute drive from Sarah.

'Yes, we can totally do that, what do you need?'

A friend of Sarah's, Melissa Bell had referred Sarah to us at Pencils Community. She had heard Micheline Andrews and a teacher, Nicole Chettle who had come to a Lions Club presentation one night and talked about the power of the pencil and what it was like for Nicole's students to have collected pencils for us the year prior. So, impressed by the presentation, she then asked whether Sarah had ever thought about taking coloured pencils over to the kids of Nepal.

In April 2015, Kathmandu and Nepal were struck by a magnitude 7.8 earthquake which killed nine thousand Nepalese and injured twenty-two thousand. The worst natural disaster to strike Nepal in over fifty years. These pencils and resources would be much needed supplies as the Nepali people rebuilt their schools and cities.

'I reckon I can take about three shoebox sizes,' Sarah told me. She had calculated that if she packed minimal clothing she could get in those extra pencils and she would jam them in tight!

We worked out that Sarah could take 10kg of pencils and stationery with her to Nepal. She would base herself in Kathmandu, leave the pencils at the hotel/tea house she was staying at and then trek to Mt Everest Base Camp. Upon her return she would hand out pencils to those in need. That way sparing her the extra 10kg of weight while trekking.

I distinctly remember the conversation that followed because in the next four hours and seventeen minutes we wrapped up what would be a life-changing conversation.

From the beginning I knew there was something very special about Sare (Sarah). I don't know if it was so much what she said but perhaps the language she used around the conversation, perhaps it was my sixth sense, but I could tell there was more going on below the surface here.

A few days later I received my first photo of Sarah and her friends at the airport via Facebook Messenger. She had decided to go on this trip when some friends at the gym said they were going on an Intrepid trek to Everest Base Camp. She was fit enough to go and decided at the age of twenty-five she should do so, see the world and explore a little.

Throughout the trip I would receive some sporadic images and descriptions to post up about Sare's journey and also some more personal messages about the insight she was gaining over there and how it was making her feel. She gave me permission to post up certain posts and photos.

The children's faces showed it all, their eyes danced, their smiles wide with happiness and gratitude. The scenery was breath-taking and all the while, all I could notice was how much Sarah's face had changed also. She had a bigger smile in every photo and every story that came through had more 'peace' in it. I know that sounds hard to describe but it was the only emotion that I could feel that summarised where she was at.

But other posts were intended just for me, as she opened up privately about her insight into the trip and how the country was changing her feelings and ask deep questions about her life. I think she must have felt like I was a lifeline back to life here in Australia, and she felt she could open up to me and share her thoughts.

'This trip changed my life,' were the first words out of her mouth as she called me from Tasmania. She had returned safely in (May 2017), well and truly bitten by the travel bug.

'But I don't know why I was able to connect with the women over there so deeply?' she questioned herself.

'I do,' I replied. We'd had enough conversations for me to piece the puzzle together.

'Because, you're a survivor,' I said. 'Just like the Nepali people, you survive every day. Existing and yet having the courage to go on. You are all vibrating at this higher frequency, I can feel it. Not quite ever coming out of that 'fight or flight' phase.

'Sarah…, do you suffer from post-traumatic stress syndrome?' I asked her, quietly.

And she was taken aback as she told me she did.

'I am a police officer,' said Sare…and 'I've booked my next trip back to Nepal already.'

It was a combination of a confession and a statement of expression all in one. I knew this, because I recognised the same feeling that I had in myself with regards to my first diagnosis. I knew that I was the person who needed to help this lovely young woman.

Sarah:

My life underwent a dramatic change at the time I met Cindy. Meeting her, and Pencils Community, coincided with an incredible and overwhelming life experience, in Nepal, of all places. This experience changed my life. Because in the two years prior to my encounter with Pencils Community and Nepal, life was very different.

I am a police officer. I have been a cop in Tasmania for four years now. I dreamed of being a police officer since the age of fourteen. I was a volunteer fire fighter since fourteen and am still to this day. Growing up, I wasn't sure if I wanted to be a fire fighter or a police officer when I finished school. Both appealed to me.

Both were exciting, challenging, purposeful, and worthwhile. And then one day, I realised – I wanted to be a cop. Because I enjoyed dealing with PEOPLE. I liked helping people, talking to people, and doing what I could to help people's lives be better. Firies helped people too, but mostly by putting water on their houses and on bushes to protect their houses. Firies spend more time in direct company with fire and water, than with people. And I know this because I've been a vollie for ten years now and enjoyed it. Firies don't do any less an important job than cops. But I wanted more of a challenge. I loved a challenge, thrived on a challenge, was somewhat addicted to challenge. But I didn't realise just how challenging it was to be a cop…

Only out of the Police Academy for 18 months, I was still fresh and still loving the job. And I loved the challenge. Upon graduating, I was posted to Burnie, in Tasmania's North West. Burnie is a small city with both country and street policing aspects.

I liked it because it was diverse and what you did from day to day varied greatly. I had my 21ˢᵗ birthday on nightshift. The Sarge brought a cake in which was very sweet and unexpected. ☺ I had a good Sergeant and a good shift, I felt lucky.

One spring afternoon in November 2015, I came to work for an average afternoon shift. At the station, there was an operation going on, conducted predominantly by the CIB (Criminal Investigation Branch), Drug Squad, and Special Operations Group. They were working to locate and apprehend a dangerous criminal that was in hiding in the vast and harsh Tasmanian North West wilderness.

Everyone knew about this guy, he was a priority target. He was actively offending and actively on drugs. He knew that the police were after him. And I'd heard that the investigators spoke to him by phone. Trying to enter into some sort of negotiation and giving him the chance to do things the easy way. But he blatantly refused to hand himself in and said he would do anything to avoid capture. Anything.

Anyway, on this day, the operation team were enlisting the help of the Uniform Section too, to boost the numbers and execute an apprehension plan. I worked in the Uniform Section – the general duties, front line, first response section. I was stoked! I loved being in on the action, doing the exciting stuff, and helping the specialist squads with jobs!! I was keen. ☺

So, I was teamed up with a drug squad member and we were given our tasks for the operation. Unfortunately, after hours of working and staking out, our man didn't pop his head up, so we ceased duties for the day. It was a bit disappointing. It would've been cool to be involved in the arrest, but it would've been even better to have him off the streets for the protection of the public. The community were getting a bit sick of him and it was up to us to catch him.

I always had a strong sense of responsibility, as a cop. I felt that, if someone was doing the wrong thing, endangering the public, or committing crime, we absolutely had a duty to do something to stop them. Sometimes we can't, or there's some things we can't help, be it because of legal constraints, time constraints, or general practicality constraints. But I always wanted to do my absolute best and to never give up until I had exhausted every possible avenue to achieve a certain outcome.

With this criminal on the run and sneaking about making victims of innocent farmers, I felt frustrated. I realised how sincerely the community out there needed us. The community were relying on us, expecting us, and hoping in us, to stop him. To protect them. Although I was not working on the task force to apprehend him, I wished and hoped and prayed the guys would get him. For everyone's sake.

The next day, I was on afternoon shift again. I was at home getting ready for work. I remember thinking about the operation, knowing that the specialist guys were planning to go out again today to try and catch him. I knew though that Uniform weren't being enlisted to help today, the bosses had mentioned. I wished we were going along to help again. Oh well. I was in my room, thinking about this when I very suddenly felt a strong urge to pray.

I am a Christian. I rarely went to church, because I worked so many weekends, and I was never one to observe any rituals or traditions or expectations of being a Christian. For me, my faith was my life. It was a lifestyle, it guided how I lived, not what I practised religiously. I did pray, but rarely knelt down or even spoke any real words, I would just sort of... think words. I would think of God and sort of send my feelings and thoughts His way, draw on the reality of who He was, and feel comforted by His presence. That's about all really.

But not this time. As I was in my room, in uniform getting ready to go, I felt a strong urge to kneel down by the bed and pray. I felt compelled to pray for the guys that were going out to apprehend the criminal. I felt so afraid for their safety... so anxious for their lives and so moved to pray for their protection.

This had never happened to me before. I mean, I prayed for my colleagues and for our safety, but not like this! I didn't know why I felt so desperate for God's protection over them on this day, or why I was crying. Yes,

I was crying, and I didn't know why. But I let the tears fall and I asked God to protect all my colleagues, my friends who were going to be out there that night, working to catch this guy and put an end to the community's angst in the area.

I didn't know if any of the guys going out were Christians, as far as I knew they weren't. But I remember thinking, God, please, for my sake, as one of your children asking You, please protect them. And that was it. I quickly wiped my tears, rolled my eyes at myself for getting all worked up before my shift and then set off to work.

I got to work, and the team were chatting about the operation, as usual. The Sergeant mentioned that we wouldn't be involved in the operation that day. Then one of the coordinators of the operation walked in to our office and spoke quietly with the Sergeant. The Sergeant nodded and then walked over to me, 'Bosch, do you want to go along with the guys today back to the bush? They need one person to take a car over. You probably won't be doing much, but they need an extra car taken over.'

Yesss!!! I thought to myself. Sure, I'll take a car over! The rest of the Constables in the office had a dig at me as I quickly packed up my computer and checked to make sure I had all my gear in my duty bag. I laughed it off and said, 'See ya's later!' I hurried out the door with a set of keys to a patrol car and joined the taskforce team downstairs. I received my instructions and we all set off.

I had no idea what I was walking into.

After meeting at the form up point and listening to our final briefing, we all split up and teamed up in groups of two, three or four, and set off to take up our positions. The Sergeant heading the operations came up to me, 'You're with me,' and he gestured to his unmarked police car.

Sure. I wasn't going to complain! I was honoured that they were enlisting me in on the plan. So, I jumped in the front seat of the Sergeant's unmarked sedan and we set off, down the quiet and somewhat creepy country roads and forestry tracks, to look for the criminal.

That was our job. To look for him. Some of the other teams had been tasked to set up in a position, or conceal themselves, or watch houses, or form a cordon. Our car had been tasked to go mobile… to look for him… to flush him out.

Another unmarked car with two experienced detectives, had also been given the task. So, we drove… silently and as covertly as possible, we peeled our way through the terrain, looking, watching, observing, thinking. Although it looked like we were doing very little, we were highly alert, our adrenaline simmering at an above average level, ready to act quickly if needed.

We knew the risks. This guy was dangerous. We knew he had a gun and suspected him to have more than one. We knew he had a stolen car. A white ute. A pretty common car! Every time we saw a white ute, we instantly scanned it to see if it was him. We were looking for a specific model though, and the stolen ute had some specific features. We knew what we were looking for. We continued to drive for about an hour, the Sergeant behind the wheel, me in the front passenger seat holding maps and keeping record of where we had been and not yet been.

Then suddenly, over the radio, a transmission from radio dispatch, saying a triple zero call had just come through from a nearby farm house. A report of a man in a white ute with a gun… the report continued… the man had just broken into a gun safe and taken a rifle and ammunition. The Sergeant stepped on the accelerator and grabbed the radio mic. Suddenly all the radios in the car, on various channels, began transmitting, constantly. The Sergeant began giving me instructions – take my phone, ring the boss, tell him this, ask him this, get this up on the map, ring this detective, answer that call. I did all this, while responding to the call on the radio. The Sergeant drove, talking on a separate radio, giving instructions, taking instructions.

We got to the farmhouse, just as another unmarked police car arrived. It was the other patrol team. We both stopped at the top of the driveway and looked down towards the house, assessing, planning. We couldn't see any white utes. The Sergeant got out of the car to talk to the other guys. One of the farmers that had called triple zero was nearby, on his phone, to police still, probably. The Sergeant began walking down to him, to get more information. Then, a white ute, bearing all the distinctive features that we memorised, slowly appeared behind a large farm shed, heading towards us up the driveway. The ute travelled about ten metres before it stopped, and slowly reversed back behind the shed.

Too late buddy, we saw you. And he saw us. Unmarked cars, dark coloured protective vests, he knew who we were. The other team quickly jumped back in their car and the Sergeant, already a way down the driveway talking to the farmer, motioned for me to bring the car down. I leaped into the driver's seat and slid the seat forward to reach the accelerator and stepped on it. The Sergeant jumped in the front passenger seat and was on the phone, talking, communicating the ute's movements while verbally formulating plans and assessing.

The ute sped off – down past the shed, down the dirt road that wound its way through the farm, down towards the paddocks. It kicked up dust and moved quick, but so were we. The other team was in front of me, in an SUV, which coped better with the potholes than our sedan. But we weren't thinking much about the potholes.

Then the dirt road ended and opened out into a paddock. It was a closed off paddock, with no way out, except the narrow gate entrance we'd just come through. The ute drove right down to the bottom corner of the paddock and stopped. He was stuck with nowhere to go. We were behind him, approaching him, closing in on him. The other team swung out to the right and we stuck to the left, to close in on him. Then the guy got out of the ute. He held a rifle.

'Stop!' the Sergeant yelled, and transmitted what we were seeing through the radio. The other team took a sharp turn and drove back the way they'd come, creating space. I stepped on the brake and stopped, as instructed, as we watched the criminal. He walked to the back of the ute and stood. He raised the rifle to his shoulder and tilted his head to look through the scope, aiming

the barrel at our car. 'Duck!' The Sergeant yelled, and we both ducked covering our heads in the car. Time stood still.

Thoughts were racing through my mind. I remembered being taught at the Academy that the best place for protection against gunfire in a car, was the engine block. A bullet can penetrate a car windscreen, a car door, pretty much anywhere through a car. But the engine block is the safest place to take cover as it can stop a bullet.

Within seconds, I was out of the car and squatting down behind the engine block, peering over the bonnet of the car. My right hand was on my Glock pistol, ready to draw. But as I peered over the bonnet, I realised we were too far to take a shot with a pistol. We were seventy metres away and Glocks were better for closer range targets. All I saw was the barrel of that rifle, pointed directly at us. Scoped, he had a much better chance of taking an accurate shot with the rifle.

I felt helpless to do anything but duck. And then there was gun fire. The splitting crack of a .22 and then a whistle as a bullet went past me. Yes, bullets whistle, I discovered in that moment. I stopped and waited to see if I felt any pain, to see if I'd been shot. No, I was okay. Then I felt absolutely sick to the core of my stomach as I thought of the Sergeant. The criminal must have been aiming for him.

The Sergeant, who I won't name, was a good friend of mine. We had always got on well and, long before today, we had formed a comradeship that I valued. Now, I felt fear and dread like I had never experienced before in my life, and I forced myself to look over to him, where I'd last seen him squatting down for cover outside the car. I prepared myself for the worst, thinking he could be dead. I looked at him, and he was okay. He was not shot. Relief flooded my body and I quickly looked back to the criminal who was working the bolt on the rifle, reloading. My heart sank... he was taking another shot. Surely, he wouldn't miss a second time. Then...silence. The rifle jammed. The criminal got back in the ute and drove through the fence, headed for the road.

'Go, go!' The Sergeant yelled. We were back in the car and gunning it back towards the road to try and stop him from getting away. Yes, he had just tried to kill us, but we HAD to catch him. It was our DUTY. We tore back up the dirt road to get around to cut him off. I drove fast. Then, over one of the radios, we heard a transmission that made us sigh with audible, tangible relief. 'He's in custody.'

There had been other police, surrounding the paddock and as he drove up onto the road, he was met by forces he could not contend with – well armed, well trained specialist police, who swiftly demonstrated their response to a criminal who had shot at police. We drove around to where the arrest had just taken place, and there was a sight I had never been so happy to see – the criminal in handcuffs on the ground, unarmed, and surrounded by police. We got him.

For an incident that unfolded in a matter seconds, it changed my life forever.

Us four from the paddock went to counselling. The police department organised debrief sessions and then we went to one-on-one counselling sessions. Although I didn't feel too bad at the time, I still went along to the meetings. But things had definitely changed in me… I was not quite the same person. For someone who was confident, outgoing, independent, and happy, I felt very little of this. Little things started happening around me and I was behaving in ways I couldn't even understand or consciously control.

Every time I saw a white ute on the road, my heart rate would rapidly rise, and my breathing would increase. I saw flashbacks of the paddock, and the feelings I felt there came back. I felt in danger and my body would start to panic. I would pull over to try and calm myself, and then try and continue with my journey.

I hated public places. Hated going out of my house. HATED going to the supermarket! I felt SO uncomfortable and anxious when I was walking through the supermarket or down the street. I felt like I had to be watching everywhere, every person all the time. And… bizarrely I would constantly be scanning for objects, places, and positions from which I could take cover from gunfire. I would think about what objects and structures around me would help protect me from a bullet and what wouldn't. Who thinks about that stuff as they walk down the street!? Me....

Sometime after I was at a friend's place, watching a movie with their whole family, who were all good friends of mine. I was enjoying it. Then suddenly one of the actors drew out a pistol and shot someone in the movie. It took me by surprise. Then I felt a sickening drop in my stomach and I couldn't see properly. My eyesight went a bit black and all I could see was the barrel of the rifle that day.

I stood up and walked out of the lounge room, out the back door. It was night time and dark. The Dad came out to find me crouched down in the driveway, breathing hard, sweating. He was very concerned for me. I just told him that the movie reminded me of a big job I had been to, was all. He was very apologetic and very supportive.

Not sleeping, not eating, and feeling emotional became the norm. Sometimes for nights in a row I couldn't sleep. I felt too anxious. And then sometimes when I did get to sleep, I would get woken up by my own tears, streaming down my face and my heart thumping. I told myself it was a normal response to an abnormal event.

But I knew I wasn't right. I felt absolutely horrible, physically, and mentally, very unsettled. So, I took myself back to my counsellor a few more times. This did help, but things still weren't quite right.

I continued working. In fact, I didn't take any time off. I wanted to still be there for the team and get on with the job. But there were a lot of triggers at work. Loud noises, too much radio traffic, and the sight of firearms instantly increased my heart rate and breathing, they all reminded me of the job.

Six months after the shooting, I went to another shooting, where one of my colleagues was forced to shoot a man running at us with a knife. I was metres away from my colleague when he drew his firearm and did what he was trained to do and forced to do in this situation. The gunshot rang out and my heart winced in pain as familiar feelings and memories shuttered through my mind.

Then about a month later I was assaulted at work by a strong, intimidating offender. He didn't hurt me physically, but he tried. He was charged. The Sergeant drove me home after that, when he found me sobbing in one of corridors. I was powerless to stop the tears... I felt violated, hurt, and unsafe. And my mind felt vulnerable all over again.

About this time, I finally got around to telling my Mum exactly what had happened. My parents knew something wasn't right, but I would just tell them that it was because I had been to a big job but didn't tell them much more because I didn't want them to worry about me. But eventually I told mum. I didn't tell Dad for about eighteen months later. Not because I didn't trust them, but because I wanted to protect them from the harsh reality of what my job entailed. But they were both very supportive, and I couldn't have got through without them. Thanks Mum and Dad. Xxx

Eighteen months ticked on and I was getting by. I was progressing forward in my work and becoming more experienced, insightful, and operationally safe and aware. Good things. Then I got accepted into the CIB and Drug Squad Course in Hobart. It was a competitive course to get on and went for six solid weeks at the Police Academy. I was honoured to be on it and was keen to learn as much as I could from it.

About half way through the course we were doing drills in the kill house (tactical training building). The drills involved wearing headgear and body armour and using Glock pistols with paint rounds in them, to shoot the bad guys (instructors role-playing). They were good drills, very challenging and life-like. But that was the problem for me... it was too much like real life.

Too many guns, too many bullets. I walked out of the kill house after completing my drill and had to sit down. One of the instructors came over and I told him I was okay, that I just needed a minute. That afternoon, after we'd finished class, I asked to speak to the course directors in private. I sat *down with the Inspector and two Sergeants who were running the course. I told them very basic details of the job I'd been to a year and a half ago and apologised for being a bit unsteady and emotional. They were very understanding and supportive. They said I didn't have to do anything that I was not comfortable doing.*

The next day we had armed offender training in the auditorium. It was a video presentation on the new training practices and policies the department was implementing. Before we went in, the Inspector came up to me as we were both heading in to the training. He told me I didn't have to watch the presentation if I didn't want to. I thanked him and said I would try to sit through it, and that I'd be okay.

The Inspector was a very good one. I had only met him a couple of times in my whole career, as we worked in completely separate sections and opposite ends of the state. But I regarded him very highly. He was one of those senior officers that I looked up to, admired, and respected greatly for his high standards, leadership qualities, and fairness. If he asked me to do something, I would do it without question.

So, I went in to the auditorium and sat with my class. My good friend, and fellow Constable from Burnie, sat next to me. She whispered to me a reminder to just leave if I felt I had to. She knew what I had been through and what I was like at the time. I nodded and appreciated her thoughtfulness. The video began to play on the big screen and the sound boomed throughout the auditorium. I watched, along with about a hundred other police officers.

Then…. shooting scenes, as I had expected, from armed offender training. But the good thing was, I thought, I was expecting it. I knew there would be gunfire, so I was preparing myself and telling my brain that it was just a video. The shooting continued, police were yelling, there was a lot of noise.

The room filled with the sounds from the re-enactments. I could feel my heart beating faster, and my breathing began to shallow and quicken.

I focused on my breathing. Breathe Sarah … I took in deep breaths, but the shooting didn't stop, and I felt emotions welling up. I closed my eyes so that I didn't have to look at the screen and focused as hard as I could on my breathing, just to try and keep it under control.

It was getting harder and harder. My stomach began to turn, and I felt light-headed. No, I was not going to walk out. I wanted to conquer this torment. A year and a half was long enough to have been plagued by memories of my past, and I was sick of it.

The loud bangs of gunfire continued to ring out and I began to feel overwhelmed. I put my head down in my hands and covered my ears, so that all I could hear was my breathing, to try and control it. My heart rate was through the roof. And through my hands, over my ears, all I could hear was gunshots. It was no good. It was just no good.

My friend put her hand on my back, 'Are you okay?' I raised my head out of my hands, unable to look at her, and stood up. I walked past my class-mates, in the row of seats next to me and down to the closest aisle. I kept my head down, hoping no one would really take much notice. I glanced up at one cop who was looking at me with the strangest look, as if I looked like a ghost. Maybe I did, I had no idea.

I walked out of the auditorium, holding my breath, not daring to breathe or think for fear that I would explode into tears and a panic attack. I walked down the main corridor, not sure where I was going, just away, as far away as I could.

I walked past the classrooms, and heard a voice behind me, 'Boschy.' I recognised it as the Inspector's voice, 'Are you okay?' I turned around to look at him; he was a good forty metres behind me, walking quickly towards me. I wanted to stop, but I couldn't. I knew that I was on the brink of complete-ly breaking down. I ignored him, regretting what I was doing, but I just couldn't stop, I needed to get out of there.

I busted through the big swinging doors at the end of the corridor to the top of the back stairwell which lead down and out of the building. I got to the top of the stairs and my feet stopped walking. I grabbed the top of the railing to stop myself from falling over and my heart exploded in overwhelming distress. I gasped for air as my throat constricted so tightly, it felt as though I couldn't breathe, and yet I was breathing so hard. I could not control it. I covered my head with my hands and began to sob. And the Inspector busted through the doors behind me.

I could barely hear what the Inspector was saying. In fact, I can only remember snippets of what he said. He stepped down a couple of stairs and looked back up to where I was clasped to the railing at the top, and he said, 'just breathe Boschy.' My mind turned back to my breathing and I forced myself to inhale. And he said, 'you're not quite right are you?' And he was right.

Within the hour, the Inspector booked me in for a meeting with the police department's best police psychologist, who was based in the city. For the next three weeks, I attended psychologist sessions two to three times a week and underwent intense treatment.

The psychologist was very good. She was highly skilled and extremely capable in her field. And she knew exactly what I needed. She explained what was going on in my mind and how my brain had stored the memories of my past. What she explained helped me to make sense of the way I behaved and responded to triggers. And she took me through a path of treatment that was one of the most challenging things I have ever had to do. She made me relive my past, fully. She guided my mind back, to feel every single emotion that I had felt back then, see everything I'd seen, hear everything I'd heard and experience everything I had experienced.

It felt extremely traumatic. Because I did relive it. Over and over. At one point, I became completely enveloped in the image in my mind, of my past ... I saw the barrel of the rifle, I felt the grass beneath my knees, I felt my hand on my gun, I heard the splitting gunshot ... and I felt a silence, a whiteness, a softness. And I had absolutely no idea what it was. Then I snapped back into reality and saw the psychologist sitting across from me, looking bewildered. She said, 'what just happened then!' I didn't know.

Initially, the treatment was almost unbearable, and then it gradually got easier. And after the treatment block, I was the best I had ever been. About two months later, I had a follow-up appointment with her. And during this session, she asked me if I believed in a God. I said I did. She said, 'I thought you might have.'

I asked her why she thought this. And she replied, 'because I saw angels, with their wings wrapped around you... twice.' I couldn't believe it. I felt quite overwhelmed, with joy. And I thought back to when she might have seen this. And then I remembered the bizarre experience I had had in her office in Hobart, when I felt whiteness and had slipped out of reality for a moment. It was when my mind was seeing him shoot at us. That was when the angels had their wings wrapped around me. And back in the paddock, when I first set eyes on the criminal and his rifle, and heard the bullet whistle past me, that's when the angels had their wings around me.

And I suddenly remembered that spring afternoon when I was compelled to pray in my room. And I realised, that I had actually prayed for my own protection. And that He had heard me.

Things were looking up for me. I continued to have semi-regular appointments with my psychologist, because I needed them, and I was pushing on. Still doing my job and still doing my best.

Thanks for the great work you are doing. These pens have either been gently used or not used at all.

Regards, Julia W.

CHAPTER 17
A Pride Is Formed

As Sarah's story came to light I just knew that we *could* and *should* do more. Her reaction, the instant feeling of connection with the Nepali people, I'd heard this before. This wasn't the first time we had heard stories like this from our returned Pencils people who had been on trips, and it wasn't even the first emergency service person we had heard this from. Yet I think it was the first time that the penny dropped for me. That we were helping the people who were *giving* the pencils as much as the child *receiving* them.

And so, an idea started to form.

Sarah:

In December 2016, one of my good friends from my gym sent me a message, saying she had a plan for her and her husband's wedding anniversary... 'I've booked a trip to Nepal to go on a guided trek to Mount Everest Base Camp! The trip is on sale with Intrepid Travel... do you want to come?' I had never been overseas before, though I had always wanted to, and I absolutely loved mountain climbing! So, I said YES!!

Before leaving for Nepal, one of my colleagues at work told me about Pencils Community. She suggested I take some coloured pencils with me to give to those in need in Nepal. I had not heard of Pencils Community before, but I loved the sound of its work and purpose. So, I called Cindy Rochstein and asked if it would be possible for me to take some pencils to Nepal.

Cindy seemed a really lovely person, genuine, and caring. She was more than happy for me to take some pencils to Nepal. I wanted to take as much as I could, so I volunteered to take 10kg of pencils and stationery items in my luggage. Cindy organised for the big load to be delivered to my house in Tasmania, through a Tasmanian Pencils Ambassador.

There were brightly coloured pencils, textas, rubbers, sharpeners, lead pencils, and more! I couldn't wait to take them over. I wasn't sure exactly where I would take them or who I would give them to, but I hoped I could give them to a group or school who needed them. I hoped very much they would be a huge help and would give children opportunities to learn and grow!

In May 2017, along with six other friends from the gym, I boarded a plane for Nepal, to climb to Mount Everest Base Camp.

I was super excited, and really not sure what to expect! We arrived in Nepal and caught a cab to our accommodation in Kathmandu. Looking out of the window of the van, I saw a very different world, different to anything I had ever seen before. A lot of people, walking around, children with no shoes on and no clothes on. Dusty streets, dark alleys, crammed stalls, and crazy traffic, I didn't know where to look! I was aware I was experiencing a bit of culture shock, but I was taking it all in and learning a lot. It was eye opening.

We had a couple of days in Kathmandu to rest from our journey and then we started our trek. We flew to Lukla, the world's most famous, dangerous airport, and stepped out into a cool, thin atmosphere, at 2,860m. I stepped down out of the small, loud aircraft, onto the tarmac. You could instantly tell the air was thinner, it felt thin as you inhaled, and it felt as though you needed to take deeper breaths to get enough oxygen. Little did we realise there was heaps of oxygen at Lukla, compared to where we were going!

Breathing in the fresh, thin air I looked up around me. Towering above me, as far as I could see, were mountains. Real mountains. Huge, snow-covered peaks, penetrating the sky and dominating the horizon in a commanding display of strength and absolute beauty. My breath was taken away and I was spell-bound for a moment. I had never been in a place this amazing before. I absorbed the experience and felt a shiver go through my body. I felt extremely fortunate to be in such a place. I felt so happy and free, for some reason, and I had not felt this in a long time.

The positive feelings were almost foreign to me and I realised this. Being the emotional person I was, a tear welled in my eye and blinked down my face. It was a tear of happiness, and I felt full of joy, wonder, and gratitude.

For the next nine days, I, along with my six friends and seven other people from around the world, trekked through the Himalayas, upwards and towards Mount Everest. We were guided by an experienced Nepali trekking leader and three experienced Nepali assistant guides. They were very good at their job. They knew the Himalayas and its risks and beauty better than anyone. They spoke good English and I learnt a lot about the Nepalese culture and way of life from talking with them.

Every day the scenery changed and continued to impress, and every day I was enraptured by the splendour of the landscape around me, and above me! On day nine, we reached Mount Everest Base Camp. A vast expanse of glacial ice and rock, the iconic campsite was a welcome sight.

At 5,365m, Base Camp was a challenge for our bodies. It was cold and there was 50% less oxygen there than at sea level. I had a bit of a headache, as did everyone else, but it was an amazing, wonderful experience and, again, I felt in awe of how blessed I was to be there.

We descended back to Lukla over three days and, after twelve days of trekking, returned to Kathmandu. We had a couple of free days there before our flight home, so we walked the colourful, intriguing streets of Thamel in Kathmandu, visited the Monkey Temple, and bought quaint gifts for our families back home. I did a bit of this, but I had something else on my mind to do…

I did not take all the pencils up to Everest Base Camp. I left them in secure storage back at our accommodation, to distribute when we got back. I mentioned to one of the trekking guides that I had brought some education supplies with me and he told me about a group called 'Seven Women'.

Seven Women was a group that provided aid and opportunities to marginalised women in Nepal by giving them skills and education that enabled them to thrive in their country, gain employment, and support their own families. They also provided aid and support to earthquake-affected areas in their country and to other families and children who were in need. This group and its purpose definitely appealed to me.

So, I donned my backpack, full of pencils and supplies, and headed off for Seven Women. The Seven Women Centre was a short drive from our hotel in Kathmandu. I arrived at the Centre and was instantly greeted by smiling, happy faces. About three women met me at the door and welcomed me in, donning my forehead with Tilaka (traditional red paste) and flower petals in my hair. I instantly felt at home.

There was a safe and beautiful atmosphere and the kind, hospitable, and loving hearts of the women was noticeable and touching. They gave me a tour of their Centre, showing me their sewing room, learning room, cooking room, living room, and crisis accommodation bedrooms. It was a beautiful big space and everywhere you looked you could see photos, flowers, handmade furnishings, and fabric.

We all gathered in a little room and I introduced myself. I tried my best to explain that I had brought some pencils and stationery items from Australia for them to keep and use however they liked. I threw the odd Nepali word in there, hoping that would help them understand me, but that just made them laugh. Who knows what I was really saying. But I gave them the pencils and their gratitude and excitement were clear.

Anita, the manager, told me that the supplies couldn't have been better timed, as they were currently working to rebuild and resupply schools that were destroyed in the 2015 earthquakes and that there were many children who did not even have one pencil with which to learn.

And I looked around at the beautiful women around me as we sat and looked at the pencils and rubbers and colourful textas, and they all had smiles on their faces. They loved it that I was there, loved it that I had taken the time to visit them, bring them pencils and sit with them, although I knew barely a word of their language and certainly nothing about them. They did not have to let me in, I had nothing to do with their lives, but they gave so much gratitude and love back to me, just as I sat there.

I saw the women who had physical disabilities and those who had had very challenging pasts and presents. And I was awestruck. Not by their appearance or situation, but by their courage. Their outstanding courage and resilience to continue living in extremely challenging conditions and to work tirelessly to help their own people and those in need, was inspiring. I left the Seven Women Centre very moved, inspired, and challenged.

As we flew back to Australia, I thought on what I had just experienced over the last three weeks. Climbing to Mount Everest Base Camp was certainly an exhilarating achievement and incredible experience. But the people of Nepal had touched me even more. Wherever I went, I saw hardship and struggle, but rising above that was resilience, hope, courage, and joy. Here were a people who had so little yet were so happy. I never knew how blessed we were in our country.

I returned to Tasmania and had to readjust to sitting on a real toilet and using taps with running water. I was grateful for my home. I returned to my job and things continued on as usual, as if I had never left.

But something was different. I was different. I had changed, yet again! But this time, in a good way!! I wasn't as irritable or angry. I started sleeping again. I felt more settled and a lot less anxious. I enjoyed being alive a lot more. And deep down I felt a passion that I didn't know I had. And that was, for the people of Nepal.

How hard was it, for me to give them a few pencils and what a difference it made!! Surely, I could do that again! We live in abundance in our lives... surely there was something I could do to help those people that I'd met, and those I hadn't met.

I called Cindy and told her what an incredible experience it was, giving the pencils to Seven Women and how much the supplies were needed over there. Cindy was so happy for me. I went on to tell her that I was feeling the best I had in a long time, since my trip. I had told Cindy previously a little of what I had been through, but I was still very private, reserved, and protective. But I told her that something had changed in me, that I had discovered a passion that I didn't know I had. And that all I could think about was how I could help the people of Nepal.

And that's when Cindy came into my life, into my heart, and into my happiness. She said, 'You can do it again. You can do whatever you want to. There is nothing stopping you from living the life you want to live.'

So, within a week of getting home, I booked another trip back to Nepal. I decided to go back, trek more in the mountains that blew my mind and to take more supplies to Seven Women. I wanted to see them again and help them. And this time, I wanted to share my passion with my friends and family and with people everywhere, to share the joy I had found and to raise money for Seven Women! I wanted other people to be happy too and to be a part of this. So together, Cindy and I created 'Project Lion Heart.'

I knew that Sarah had a great connection with Melissa and I with Micheline, so we decided to all have a group Skype call one day. Now, I don't know about you but when you put four amazing people together in conversation, then amazing things can happen. Between catching up and loads of laughter we somehow coordinated a massive pilot program that we entitled: Lion Heart. With our tag line or motto: Courage to thrive.

The team consisted of myself as Lion Heart Project Manager, Sarah as Lion Heart Ambassador and liaison to the Tasmania Police and other emergency services, Melissa Bell as our Lions Club Vice-President and our amazing logistics, finance and operations manager and Micheline Andrews, our existing Pencils Community Tasmanian Ambassador and project coordinator.

Up until now, the focus had very much been on the person receiving the pencils, the child receiving the goodies. Sarah's experience highlighted to all of us what an impact the simple act of giving can have on our Pencils Ambassadors.

For the past two years we had gone from one messy desk and Facebook post to hearing the same story over and over again. That people feel good about themselves when they give the pencils, and as such, Pencils encourages a healing pathway for all.

Right the way back to our original fireman who said he could take pencils, to all the individuals we had met along the way, teachers, midwives, parents and not knowing all their own personal stories but understanding that we had a far greater impact than we had ever imagined. Then along came Sare, who was bravely able to stand before us and say, 'I have PTSD, and Pencils changed my life and helped me heal.'. And from then on Project: Lion Heart was born.

Thank you so much for coming to our school and spending time with the children. I can tell you we had very positive feedback after you left. You really inspired them all, even the students who would not normally 'engage' were hanging off your every word. Thank you for the education in Pencils and sustainability. We can't wait to start our collection for you.

Jenny

CHAPTER 18

Project: Lion Heart - Courage to Thrive

Project: Lion Heart is a humanitarian mission for individuals to embark on a personal journey through giving. We are made up of two amazing community organisations that have come together to form a partnership: City of Burnie Lions Club and Pencils Community, in order to create an ongoing opportunity for an individual to be part of a humanitarian mission to help other communities.

This is the first time Project Lion Heart has existed and our focus for 2017 was on Sarah Bosch returning to Nepal to help with projects on the ground. Our aim was to make this project available one day on an ongoing basis to other individuals.

Lion Heart focuses on championing our service personnel as well as mental health and of course Pencils Community. Our aim in doing this is to be able to assist individuals and community groups by raising awareness and education, sustainability, humanitarian issues, and how to talk openly about mental health.

Our experience with Lion Heart made us recognise the importance of reducing the stigma around our emergency services personnel and mental health. We always think of these people as being tough and

191

resilient, when in fact, we are all human, we all experience challenges in life and seek healing, connection and love.

So, one day in August 2017, four months after talking to Sarah, we boarded a plane for Tassie. I took Olive out of school knowing that the experience would be an education in itself. We packed our ski jackets and also our bathers as we were going from snow to sun (finishing our roadshow with four days of R&R in sunny Queensland).

It took approximately ten weeks to bring the project together. All of us working long days and late nights fuelled with a belief that we could do more. We put together a series of back-to-back events that involved speaking at schools, a soiree launch event, media interviews, Scout sorting pencils days, Father's Day BBQs with the local fire brigade, police station visits, lunch with Mates 4 Mates culminating in a huge Services Clubs Dinner on our final night. We held raffle prizes and competitions, face painting, and more. It was a ten-day no-holds-barred rock star tour and we really smashed it.

We existed on almost no sleep, piled into and out of the car in our snow jackets and drove from the northwest coast of Tasmania backwards and forwards to Launceston, via Devonport, with our great friend Kaz, filming every step of the way. We met hundreds of children with whom we had an opportunity to share the story of Pencils and Lion Heart and share Sarah's personal story. We totally killed ourselves from an energy perspective, not one of us escaping illness in some form or another on the trip. But it was worth it.

Sarah:
Project Lion Heart was all about having courage to thrive! That's our tagline – Courage to Thrive. Because life is very short. Life can be taken from you by one bullet, one accident, one sickness, one turn of events. We know not the day or the hour. And life was meant for more than just survival. You can thrive in life!! But this takes courage. Because, everyone goes through difficult times.

Everyone experiences moments in their life where their ability to function or smile is severely curtailed by pressure, stress, or by traumatic events. And to move past that, and do things even though it's so hard, is brave. It takes courage to take a step forward, when it hurts. It takes courage to face your past, and your fears. It takes courage to thrive.

But when you give something to someone, you get something back. Giving the pencils to Seven Women, for them to give to children so that they could learn to read and write, gave me even more back.

Lion Heart became a project not just about helping those on the receiving end, but about helping the GIVERS. Lion Heart was a mission to help those suffering from post-traumatic stress, or other mental health challenges, to have courage and to give them support and opportunities to give, and to find their passion in life.

Project Lion Heart championed emergency service workers, military, service people, and anyone who worked in a high stress environment. It is open for anyone, mums and dads included!

For a new project, we had to have a launch!! So, in September 2017, Cindy and her family flew down from Melbourne to launch Lion Heart. We packed as many school visits, pencil collections, talks, and fundraising events into a week as we could. What a huge week! The City of Burnie Lions Club were an amazing support – they helped out at all our fundraising events, put on barbeques, ran raffles, and collected funds. Cindy and I visited several schools, talking about Pencils Community and how pencils created a way for me to find a new passion.

Schools everywhere collected up pencils and stationery items and gave them to us. Then we had a big community pencil-sorting day where people could come along and learn how to sort and package pencils for Nepal and to talk about Lion Heart and the meaning behind it. It was a great opportunity to meet new people who were living with similar challenges or who had similar passions, and to be able to build a connection and friendship that meant we were not alone in the hardships we faced in life.

Our final Project Lion Heart event was a dinner, held at the Burnie RSL who had been very supportive of the Project. Other service club representatives came, along with friends, family, and colleagues. Cindy spoke first about Pencils Community and how her own personal challenges had given birth to the amazing cause and charity of Pencils Community. The plan was then for me to talk about my personal story and how that had created Project Lion Heart. I had talked about Nepal and Project Lion Heart several times by that point, at schools and other group gatherings. But I hadn't really shared my personal story in public before.

I was very nervous. I knew that my mind hated talking about what had happened to me and how it affected me. I didn't mind speaking in public, but I always found it so hard when I started breaching the topic of the shooting and my struggle to move on from it. But I wanted to do it. I knew I had to do it. More for myself than anyone else.

The week-long launch of Project Lion Heart had been exhausting. Cindy and I, and Mel from Burnie Lions, had barely slept all week as we planned and organised all the events. And for the most part I wasn't thinking about why I was actually doing it, because I was so focused on running the events. But deep down, I knew I was doing it so I could move forward, so I could hold on to what I loved and was passionate about, and to help others to have courage too. So, the night of the dinner, when I would finally share my story, was a big moment for me.

I stood on stage and began telling of how I had trekked in Nepal and met beautiful people at Seven Women. I told of how I had given them pencils and how rewarding that was. And I started to share about how much this experience had helped me and how it had given me a new perspective on life. 'Because,' I said, 'things were very different for me before.' I told everyone I was a police officer and that, about two years ago my life was almost taken. And that after that… life looked very different, and I was not the same person anymore… My voice trailed off and there was silence. I could not speak. Overwhelming emotions of intense hurt descended on me and I fought back to keep it away. I knew this would happen! I concentrated on breathing and told myself I was not walking away. I was going to get through this. I closed my eyes and waited for the wave of memories and emotion to pass. I took a deep breath and continued on. I explained as best I could, and as my body would allow, what happened to me.

I then began talking about the new passion I had for Nepal. My heart instantly lifted, and I could not wipe the smile from my face as I talked about the people of Nepal. I told of my plan to go back, to raise money for them, and my new desire to help others find the same joy and passion that I had. My speech ended on a positive note and I was happy that I got through it. I was proud of myself for surviving my first re-telling of my personal story in public. The whole thing was captured on video by my good friend Kaz and is now uploaded to the Lion Heart Courage Facebook Page, for anyone to watch.

I stepped down off the stage and into Cindy's waiting embrace. She was so proud of me and I was so grateful for her support. Then I quickly slipped away to the girls' bathrooms, sat on a bench in there and fell apart. What I had just done had taken so much energy and effort, it had left me exhausted. The strength it took to hold it together and verbalise what I had been through and how it made me feel every day was debilitating. My heart was aching. I just waited. Waited for it to pass like I had done so many times before, and eventually there were no tears left to fall. But I had done it.

I had done it.

I take the microphone and step onto the stage. I had saved my most difficult talk till last. I opened with how we had met and how the project had come together. What events we had participated in along the way and what we had learnt. There were things I wanted to say and so I saved them for my final part of my talk. I knew it would rattle some cages but still it had to be said and delivered.

I didn't want to hurt Sarah along the way but the act of working with many organisations meant there were ways in which we could say things and ways in which we couldn't; it was about not being seen to be endorsing anything or saying it in the politically correct way.

But in doing this we were fuelling the very stigma we were trying to avoid. Stigma that at this pointy end of the discussion costs lives. People could kill themselves if we spent all our time, saying what needed to be said but not saying it at all, too afraid to speak and open up. I began my final comments…

I want to thank Tasmania Police, Lion's Club, and all the organisations that have supported us, for giving us the opportunity for open dialogue. It's by sweeping the issue under the rug, that creates and feeds the stigma. When you feed the stigma, when you silence the discussion, you indirectly contribute to blocking the pathway for our amazing and respected people to heal. Let's face the fact, when you feed the stigma, you cost lives.

For those that ask me who am I to talk about this, my answer is…who aren't I? I am the Founder and CEO of Pencils Community, with my mission to help children colour their world. I am not an expert on PTSD, we have experts, psychologists, doctors and programs but it is not difficult to see that Pencils has offered a vehicle for change within the individual and change with stereotypes of our service personnel.

When we dug deeper into this conversation there was so much Political Correctness about what words I could and couldn't use, and I remember throwing my arms in the air and saying, why are we making it so hard to talk about this? I'll tell you why? It's fear.

The room is silent at this point.

Because nobody wants to say the wrong thing. However, by dotting our 'I's and crossing our 'T's, by trying to get the discussion perfectly right, we are missing the main message.

That there are people in our community who need our support, connection, and love. We need to be talking about this and coming up with more and better solutions and pathways, not furthering to destroy lives. As our great friend Dion Jensen, who is an expert in PTSD explained to us, it is acceptance, not judgement that is required.

Stunned faces look back at me as I am able to say what isn't being said.

That by trying to always do the 'right' thing or say the 'right' thing, we are indirectly covering this up and costing lives. Every one of us in this room.

Pencils Community has created one pathway for healing through Project: Lion Heart, and you can hear that through Sarah's personal story. And we hope to continue these projects, with as many people as we can, because in the end it's about the person giving, and the person receiving.

When you are left with a decision between love and fear, we are going to choose love every time. That's what we do at Pencils.

We raised $3,000 for Sarah to take back with her to Nepal, specifically to help with some grass-root education projects being run through the Seven Women Foundation, headed up by Founder Stephanie Woollard.

Intrepid Travel Group, also big supporters of Seven Women, matched our fundraising dollar for dollar. In the end Sarah revisited Nepal with $6,000, spoke to the women and families whom she met the first time and gave them pencils too. She also took part in a cooking program that helped marginalised Nepali women to retrain and become independent.

Sarah:

A month later I flew back to Nepal, the country I had fallen in love with, full of its people of courage and strength that were now my best friends, and with its mountains that left me breathless every day.

This time I trekked fifteen days with Intrepid through the Annapurna Region, to an altitude higher than Everest Base Camp. At the top of the Pass, the highest point, my heart skipped several beats and I was flooded with an exhilaration that I had only experienced once before - when I was in Nepal last time, at Lukla airport.

It was the same feeling. I was filled with awe and joy as my eyes beheld the shimmering, majestic Himalayas. Snow-capped, exposed, raw, and steadfast, each peak was a masterpiece of its own and together, they formed a silent orchestra playing a perfect melody into an atmosphere where the acoustics struck the very deepest part of your soul. For me anyway. Here, was my favourite place.

I also returned to Seven Women and delivered another 10kg of donated stationery items from local Tasmanian schools and told them of all the money we had raised for them. They were so happy and so appreciative. It was good to see them all again. They had the same beautiful smiles and hearts and welcomed me into their home as if I was one of their own. We cooked together, played together, and chatted. I helped draw up a document on one of their old laptops to record all the items in their shop that they had made to sell. I spent two days with them, helping them, and sharing with them. It was a really special time and my friendship and bond with them was strengthened. As was my passion to help them and be a part of the beautiful, selfless, and courageous work in which they thrived.

*This second trip to Nepal was even better than the first, which I didn't think could be possible! But it was even more wonderful. I returned home after my three weeks there and I was **happy**. I knew then that I had found my passion again, and that it was there to stay. My confidence, independence, and outgoing spirit had returned, and the pain of the past no longer haunted me. And Lion Heart was established.*

Most of all Sarah had begun to really turn a corner in herself and her recovery from PTSD. She had gone from being in a state of struggle, to being able to stand in front of one hundred people and tell them what had happened to her. From that moment she felt the bullet rush past her head and her blood drain from her soul, to the reignition of her hope and love for life again in Nepal with the Nepali people and the rebuilding of her life as she knew it now. This was her new normal.

After such an amazing time in Tassie, we barely leave.

Such an expenditure of energy results in a last minute medical emergency for me. With a tachycardia heart rate of over 200bpm and feeling so very unwell due to an allergic reaction to some of my new medication, we somehow boarded the plane to Melbourne and made our way eventually to Queensland later that day. I barely remember any of the travel, yet to say it took all my courage to get there and not be in a local hospital somewhere.

It had been a phenomenal effort from all of us. I felt like all of us had stepped from the cold and dark snow-covered field in Tassie into the heat and light of the afternoon sun of Queensland. Our minds awakened to the issues and forging a pathway into health and happiness. It truly felt like stepping out of the dark on this issue of PTSD and mental health for Sarah, for our team and with our new understanding to step into the light.

Sarah has returned from her second trip to Nepal. She has a two-day stay over with us on her way back home to Tassie. We pick up from the airport one very jet-lagged and emotional girl. She is heartbroken to leave her love, Nepal. Teary, sick, and exhausted. We nurture her as best as we can with food and care. I pack into her bag Dion's book, 'The Good News about PTSD' and tell her to read it – his 'speak', his 'language' will resonate strongly with her as both have been police officers. I am concerned that this trip has been another trigger for her PTSD.

After 48 hours we travel back to Melbourne's Tullamarine Airport with Sarah to return home to Tassie. I feel relieved and happy when I hear that Sarah and Dion have made a connection through Facebook and Dion's book. It had the impact on Sarah that I hoped it would and she finds her feet again in no time, this time creating bigger plans for her future.

I love that our 'Canoefleet' is growing daily, as we may have different missions in life, but we all have a common purpose to change and save lives.

The next week I see Dion, I load him up with pencils that have come via another author to Ocean and then onto Dion. As we wave goodbye to Dion at the airport in Queensland, Ocean and I give each other a smile, we know that Dion has just become our second International Lion Heart Ambassador. And days later he sends back photos of his visit to an orphanage in Indonesia, all 6ft 4 of him standing twice the height of these children as he gives out our pencils, creating hope and opportunity for the children he meets. The Lion Hearts are beginning to roar!

Hearing you speak out about PTSD in emergency services encouraged me to take action for myself. I have long suffered but am self-diagnosed. I was inspired to hear that people in our community are beginning to understand more of what we are going through and more of what we need.

So, thank you.

Anon Midwife xx

CHAPTER 19

Roarrrr

'I'm in a tent camping with the kids,' as the text message from Sarah comes through. It is January 2018 and we have of course kept in touch ever since. We are like giggly schoolgirls catching up!

'I'm coming to Melbs for three days to see you Cin, I have so much to tell you about Nepal and Lion Heart,' says the next message.

And there in the mountains of Tassie, in a tent late at night, a flight to Melbourne is booked and Sare arrives on my doorstep a week later.

In typical 'us' style we cram in as many meetings as possible. The first day we spend hours packing pencils and stationery ready for our delivery to Intrepid Travel Group in the city the next day. And during that first night we hold a Lion Heart strategy meeting – where to now?

On little sleep the night before, we stay up talking outside under the stars about life moving forward.

The next day we are up early and into the car for the next adventure. I apologise in advance for swear words that may occur while trying to park in the city. Not at the parking complexes but on the street, in a loading zone with fifteen minutes to unpack a car full of pencils. Somewhere, in the middle of Melbourne with back-to-back hook turns we find a carpark almost opposite where we need to be – this is almost unheard of in Melbourne CBD. (*For those not from Melbourne hook turns are right hand turns from the left-hand lane on the amber or red traffic light – no one really knows, so everyone just toots their horns and I've spent the majority of my life in Melbourne!*)

We unload the car and meet our friends from Intrepid Group Headquarters (Melbourne). We have donated them pencils for their staff to take over to India and Nepal as they regularly travel as part of their work. Sarah and I are happy to have met the team here but sensing Sarah's 'fish out of water' feeling we leave and settle in for a quick lunch.

We then have the pleasure of catching up with our good friend Michael Gallus from Footys4All as I wanted him to meet Sarah. With promising talk on the horizon, we enjoy a jovial catch up and we are on our way. Michael is always so much fun to be around and it is amazing to have our charities all begin to connect into one to become a stronger force.

Although weary from the day, we manage to have another heart to heart on the way home. Knowing each other so well we are comfortable talking about everything and it is so lovely that we both feel we have each other's support always.

The afternoon finishes with a meeting with Val and Jaime (SANCSS) and the tribe has met. Later that night we continue our discussion of Lion Heart moving forward and all that entails. It's time to grow more. Sarah will become the CEO of Lion Heart and take the 'Pride' forward with our support.

Sarah:

As I write now, it has been just three months since my second trip. It has not been a year since I first went to Nepal. And it has been only five months since Lion Heart was launched. But how far it has come. Here, now, is the first time I have written my personal story in any detail. It's been hard. I've had to stop several times to take rests, and even days away from it to give my heart a break.

It is all very real, very raw, and very impacting for me. Although I speak of the pain of my past as if it is long gone, the effects of what happened are with me every day. I still have hard days, but now I have something wonderful and beautiful to think about and channel my energy into.

I am now the CEO of Lion Heart and I have an amazing team around me. My vision for the future of Lion Heart is tremendous. I have a great desire to help my colleagues who suffer the same torment and sadness from the job, that I did, and I so badly want them to find their passion in life too. I want fire fighters, police officers, and ambulance officers to feel safe, valuable, and happy. I want teachers, nurses, doctors, vets, and receptionists to have a purpose in their life that makes their job not hurt so much. I want builders, plumbers, scientists, and managers to reinvigorate a passion that they once had. I want mums, dads, sisters, brothers, grandmas, and grandpas to experience life in abundance. I want people everywhere, all over the world, to have courage to thrive.

I really don't care if that sounds ridiculous or unrealistic or silly. I really don't care. Because there are people out there, like me, who have experienced a low in their lives that constricts the very breath from their lungs and all they want in life is to be able to live again. I know there are hearts out there aching; hearts in uniform and not in uniform. And I want those people to know that they are not alone. I want them to meet Lion Heart and be a part of the support and opportunities that it can provide. I want them to overcome their fears, face their past, their present and their future, and choose to really live life. I want them to have courage to thrive.

I would just like to thank Cindy for the opportunity to tell my story, and for being the inspirational, courageous, caring, and amazing person that she is to me. You are one of the biggest blessings in my life. I would like to thank my mum and dad, brothers, and sisters for always being there for me and for understanding me. I love you all very much. I would like to thank my psychologist, Julie, for her patience, insight, and care. You are a true lifesaver. I would like to thank my Sergeant, Sergeant Turale for the countless hours he has spent listening to me and supporting me. You will never know how much I appreciate you. I would like to thank Senior Sergeant Conroy for being there for me since day dot. You are my role model. I'd like to thank my friend Octopus (it's just a nickname) for being my soul buddy. You have been there for me through all my highs and lows and have taught me the meaning of true friendship. And finally, I'd just like to thank God for protecting me, sheltering me, and never leaving me. You are my rock, and my fortress, and my deliverer; my God, my strength, in whom I will trust; my buckler, and the horn of my salvation, and my high tower. Psalm 18:2.

What lies ahead for Sarah is the dream and the life that she has always wanted. Yet to get there she has looked deep into her life and questioned every value she has ever had. Reflected over every moral decision and boundary to achieve a new gauge reading on where she stood. Because she is different than the person she was before this happened. This life event, trauma and experience that resulted from it, in Nepal.

Sarah has had to critically re-evaluate her life and transform herself. She has had to dig deep into her psyche, find the courage and continue to live her life. She is learning what she wants, and she is having faith and courage every day. She has earned her title as CEO of Lion Heart many times over.

Dearest Cindy,

I wanted to send you a letter ages ago, as soon as you left even, but I've finally sat down to say something I really wanted to tell you.

Meeting you, has changed my life. I could never have dreamed where that phone call would lead.

Project Lion Heart is the biggest and most meaningful, hardest and most beautiful thing that I've ever been a part of. And it would not have been without you.

You have encouraged me to step out and beyond, further than I dreamed. You have supported me to overcome my fears and past, to have courage. I always had a relentless drive and passion in me that I just wanted to express and discover, but I didn't think anyone else saw it or could tell. But you could.

Thank you for giving so much of yourself, for my sake. Thank you for coming to Tasmania to launch Lion Heart. Thank you for sacrificing your family, your needs, and your sleep!!

No matter what the future holds, I will never forget every moment we spent together, and you, will always have a very special place in my (Lion) heart. Thank you, Sarah Grace xx

CHAPTER 20

Meditating on the Mountainside with Purpose and Perspective... kind of...

In the lead up to Christmas (2017) I'm oscillating somewhere between trying to push mentally through a bought of pneumonia and faint in the pencil room. Melbourne has given us yet another thirty-five degrees humid day and although I am sick and have just lost most of my sight overnight, we are packing an emergency shipment of two hundred pencil cases for some gorgeous kids in the Solomon Islands for our friend Karla (Friends of Brilliant Star).

We had previously sent pencils to the Solomon Islands (and also PNG) with a contact of ours Michelle Behsman in Cairns. Michelle had called us one day and explained that a group of her friends were travelling together and had offered to pay for the postage if we could send some pencils her way. We sent nearly 40kg of supplies to her and her friends, who later took the pencils on their trip and gave them out to the very grateful and excited children.

The school at Friends of Brilliant Star have a school made of natural timbers and the roof is made of leaves. With only half a roof, when it rains their schooling must stop. There is a blackboard with no chalk and two hundred kids with no pencils! Yet a beautiful husband and wife team home-schooled their children, then some more children in the village, and from then on, a small school began.

Our gorgeous friend and contact, Karla (from Friends of Brilliant Star) supports this school offsite from regional Richmond in Qld. She's an amazing lady in her sixties who is a kindred spirit and a sufferer of arthritis and chronic pain and shows that you can still help children around the world even if you live remotely. She regularly visits the Solomon Islands, feeling charged up and empowered when she is there, only to fall in a heap afterwards. That sounds familiar. That's our roller-coaster ride.

After packing twenty-five pencil cases and shaking, I lie down on the concrete floor. Feeling so unwell is just shit. It's hard work and the only lesson I hear is the same one in my head every day, balance vs endurance. It is a tenuous balancing act between life and health versus being propelled by your purpose and enduring the pain.

You see, even if I rest and do gentler activities, I am still sore. So, I figure I may as well achieve what I want to, because it all hurts anyway right?

The lesson is somewhere in that middle space, I'm yet to find the correct balance, but I'm trying to, all the time. I am torn because when you know you can help and make a difference to a child's life, you want to keep going! And well, life can be short... I get reminded of that often. That we all have an expiry date, mine just might be a little closer than first planned.

My theory is that you really can't take all these medications and inject your body with all these things to suppress your immune system... and really expect to get away with it, right? I mean I already proved that theory recently with my diminished eyesight being a side effect of my Biologic injections. In a space of a month I have battled an atypical pneumonia, cortisone injection that went haywire, numb face for a week, allergic reaction to antibiotics, withdrawals from having to come off my normal medications and loss of eyesight. This was just the 'new' stuff on top of my normal, but new pain being introduced takes a while for the old and new pain to learn to get along nicely – it's fair to say they aren't friends at first!

Fortunately, a combined effort between Jules in Melbourne and Flash in Brisbane, and somehow, we manage to coordinate a courier delivery, a car ride and a container shipment over one of the more difficult times of the year to get things done – the week between Christmas and New Year.

It takes a community, right? I am so grateful for everyone's help – even though I struggle to ask for it when I am really sick. I know people want to help and I think part of it is because Pencils IS such a simple concept.

The pencil represents what we as a community is all about. If you look at an actual pencil, it is about taking the 'eraser' part of the pencil and erasing helplessness, hopelessness, poverty, negating cycles of violence, gang behaviour, and abuse. On the other side of the pencil is the pointy graphite lead or creation part. The graphite represents the ability to create hope and opportunity, to draw, create, read, and write, to become educated, to rise above social, racial, and political injustice and create real change to the world as we know it.

'Give children an education and you give them a life' said young mathematics teacher Eddie Woo (Local Australian Hero of the Year 2018). And he was 100% right!

I know it may seem like I am being all preachy to you – I'm not. I have identified some insight that I hope will help, both you and me.

I'm not sitting here on the mountain side meditating; the truth couldn't be further from this.

You see, a few days after Christmas, I have a big rare block of time on my hands to ponder and think about life and about Pencils. I **have**

to. I am watching the discs spin in the CT Scanning machine as I lie immobilised with a massive needle hanging outside my shoulder joint. The longer I stay still and don't move, the quicker this process will be. And thinking about Pencils and life is distracting me.

As the silver discs spin I try to find a relatable sound to take my mind off it. Is it like a food processor? No not that loud, it's more like a loud hum. I fail dismally at turning my mind off, anxious about this new procedure being put on me at last minute. It's supposed to be more precise about getting the injection directly into my joint and therefore more accurately pinpoint the damage.

I move my agitation to a blob of paint on the roof. Insignificant to all who come in and out of the room, the doctors, the nurses, but not the patients. I bet many have looked up to that blob of paint willing a procedure to hurry up or be different. I feel I have stared at a lot of blobs of paint in my time, too many to count. They seem to help at the direct moment a needle goes in. This time the experience however feels more traumatic.

The doctor used his full body weight to push the needle deep into my shoulder joint. I feel like I have been stabbed into the depths of my shoulder with an icy needle, because that is exactly what happened. The weight pushes my shoulder deeper into the trolley bed of the CT Scan. Medicine feels so mechanical and butchery at times, and still I stare at the spot.

I feel for the doctor; I know what it's like to inject myself each week with my Biologic injections. Sometimes it feels like you are squeezing thick glue through the tiniest of needles. The worst is over he tells me as the anaesthetic permeates my arm. It spreads across my chest and up my neck to my face, tingling along the way. Almost like tiny electrical currents as they ignite the nerves as the anaesthetic glides through.

Some more talking and dabbing and now the next needle is ready. This time I can sense an object in my shoulder, I can clearly see the needle sticking out as I reverse backwards and forwards into the CT Scanner until the exact spot is sighted and the medicine can do its job. I choose not to look. I'm not squeamish with these procedures now, there have been too many.

The doctor turns to me and reassures me, telling me how good I am at being very still. I have learnt in these moments that the blob of paint is my cue to let go. Of everything. To let go of fighting this disease every second of every day, let go of the pain and let go of my control. In these moments I have implicit trust in my doctors to do their magic.

Ten more minutes pass and I am allowed to sit up. The nurse says to me, 'You can move your arm now,' but it lays there, sort of limp. I've achieved my 'walking meditation trick' of being able to turn a body part into a piece of wood so I can't feel it be traumatized. I will it to move and grab my bag with my other hand and protect and hold my shoulder like it's a broken arm.

I am guided to the change rooms and instructed that once I have changed I need to wait in the waiting room for twenty minutes, 'in case' I have a reaction. I take a quick photo of the assault of my shoulder in my hospital gown, thinking that the designs of the gown are getting way better and ergonomic. The strap that does the gaping back up is now attached at the front with a seam, right over the belly button. The straps don't fall off now and there is no struggle to get it off. Getting re-dressed on the other hand takes some skill, and I struggle through and take a seat in the waiting room.

A few more people come in for procedures but it's towards the end of the day, the day before a long weekend. I curse myself that the appointment is so late, knowing I will now have another sleepless night from the side effects of the injection. Awesome, not really.

I seem to not be able to escape sleepless nights right now as I still struggle through my pneumonia infection cough. I really wish I could give my ol' body a rest, but still tell it secretly that it is doing great

213

standing up to this repetitive madness. 'You're tough, you can do this, you know what to do,' I tell it through my ESP or inner voice. It doesn't respond, it just is.

The nurse and reception staff keep an eye out for me, and I'm glad. To be honest I feel quite dazed; is my mind trying to process the last two hours? I touch the left side of my face. My left shoulder is the one feeling stabbed, so it is the same side. My face feels a little numb and tingly. I'm so dazed that I don't react straight away, normally I would be like, 'Fuck, what now? Really?' but instead I am willing it to go away. Like a scared little girl about to get in trouble. After fifteen minutes, the tingly and numbness has spread to my entire left face, the left side of my lips and my tongue.

As I approach the desk to let them know, I tell them it's a mild reaction. This is true, I know my breathing is fine and my pulse feels normal. They tell me they will need to call the doctor back. He's left for the day, they smile and say, better that you said something, it's a long weekend. In my mind, I am ambivalent to the day in the calendar, health stops for no diary or occasion, it does what it wants when it wants.

I sit back down as the conversation relays through, 'Is she breathing?' 'Yes.' 'Is she sitting upright?' I can tell the questions from the other side of the phone call… 'Yes, she's upright!'

Surreal. And then the receptionist informs me that the doctor will turn his car around and come back for an assessment.

I sit alone in the waiting room. Other than the odd whirl past of a receptionist every few minutes I feel alone. *I hope I don't just drop here and stop breathing, no one would bloody find me for minutes!* As the thought becomes a more anxious one, I try to calm myself down. I cast my mind back to this morning's activities.

My daughter and I took our two dogs out for a walk. We have one older Border Collie, 'Jordie' and now a new little 'wuppy' as we call her, 'Maple' because she looks the same colour and is as sweet as Maple Syrup.

She is a Kelpie X Boxer and is gorgeous. We lost our old Dvee-girl (my beloved Staffy) five months prior, due to old age. It was a heart-breaking end as they all are when you are so close to your fur babies.

Time marched by and Jordie was quite mopey. Having lived with Dvee for twelve years, he didn't know what it was like to be alone. So, we decided to get a puppy for Xmas, or as timing would have it, just before Xmas. Rescue pups don't come on demand, and so the beautiful twelve-week old Maple entered our life and our hearts.

On this morning my daughter, Olive and I took the puppies out for three small blocks walk. This is what I can manage on a good day at the moment, so I still try to get out and do it. We meander along, more interested in our own conversation and we decided to let the puppies explore a little more on lead rather than enforcing the 'heel' training today.

We laughed as 'Maply-Moo' trots past a semi-trailer truck parked on the side of the road. She's all paws at present as she grows and often reminds me of a reindeer or pony prancing along. Suddenly she catches her reflection in the ginormous wheels and gets a fright. Her head was huge and quite possibly unrecognisable to her in that moment until she had several other, closer inspections. Nothing was said but my daughter and I saw the exact same moment at the exact same time and we looked at each other and giggled. It was a sweet highlight of our walk, and one in which I reflect back on now.

It's funny how in times of stress you can take your mind back to a moment and try to not overact. These moments kept me calm until I was, for the third time, reminded by the reception staff that it was a long weekend. The doctor arrives back.

I was taken back to the examination room where all my vitals were checked. The doctor was satisfied that it was most likely the anaesthetic but to call him in three hours if the numbness persisted. I drive myself home, hoping I am okay and ten minutes later make it back through the door, greeted by concerned looks and a smiling daughter happy to have me back. It's these moments that remind me of how 'normal' our lives are and that they are made up of tiny inconsequential moments that make up an even bigger energy, of love. It was their love that got me through today.

Three hours pass, and I still can't feel the left side of my face. I decide to go to bed and try the old-fashioned approach of some rest. And some painkillers. A few hours later, I am up with some dramatic electrical cramp radiating through my entire back and want to vomit. Thankfully, this one passes after twenty minutes and I go back to bed to find my own blob of paint on my ceiling to stare at for a while.

The morning arrives, the numbness is still there in my face and neck. My shoulder feels more like a hot dagger has been stabbed into it this time rather than an icy cold needle, but this type of pain is easier to manage. Hot packs and pain relief are the order of the day, with coffee.

Mum arrives over to take the pressure off entertaining Oli on school holidays and we agree that as the numbness hasn't progressed that a few days of rest and relaxation might be the best thing for me. We have made decisions like this in the past and always been right, we know my body has a huge limit as to exactly how many drugs you can throw at it. Saturation Level reached. A day in bed, and we just hope our 100% medical evaluation of me is still up to scratch.

Knowing thy ledge is an important self-evaluation, reflective statement. I know my obstacle and ledge is a physical one foremost. The ability for my body to try and keep up with the pace of my mind and purpose, my ambition. Well sometimes an assaulted shoulder, numb face, and dumb pneumonia creep in instead and force me to slow down. So, you could say that 'Balance' in life in general is my hardest lesson to learn.

It is only now that I know that my time could be limited, I mean how many more walks with my daughter and the puppies do I have left in my life before all is said and done? I realise that through every experience that I can see and be reminded of the same lesson. That purpose and ignition of one's soul is an energy and light that will continue to burn. I will remember the walks with my daughter, the way her eyes light up as she giggles, and she will remember she was surrounded by love. I'm not gone yet and quite frankly don't plan to be for a long time yet, but throughout my disease I get constant reminders and lessons that if I am going off track, that I get a gentle nudge back onto my path.

I look down at the silver-copper ring on my hand. It has changed to a more copper, rose gold tone from the CT Scanner experience. It shows me that change happens all the time, sometimes subtly like my ring, like our walk, or sometimes obviously and abrasively, such as my shoulder, face, and eyes. And change is what we need to have in order to continue our path of knowledge. It's about lessons learnt and knowledge gained.

I don't think that's too preachy? I hope not anyway.

Just wanted to let you know that you're awesome, amazing, and beautiful. I totally love everything that you are and everything that you stand for. And, I am absolutely stoked to be a part of your Pencils Community. Can't wait to help you change this world!'

– Jason Smith (aka FLASH);
Brisbane Ambassador

CHAPTER 21
What's Next?

At the beginning of 2018, we receive our long awaited official Charity Status. It took weeks of paperwork (yes, they really mean it will take weeks of paperwork) and we set out to complete our required documentation. Never ever get an author (let alone two authors) to fill in paperwork, every question becomes a life story and essay rather than a concise answer. I learnt this the hard way! We saw a lawyer and got our systems lined up and we became an Australian legal charity.

We also set up our official bank account at our local Commonwealth Bank Branch in Seaford (Victoria). 'Nags' who assisted us in setting up our official bank account heard about the story of Pencils. He must have put in a good word because a few weeks later, the manager 'Greg' rang us and offered us a $500 Community Grant donation and said that he would go to the local Officeworks to buy whatever items we needed.

He delivered them personally and arrived with boxes of new solar powered calculators (we can't send calculators with batteries because if you think pencils are a luxury imagine what batteries would be!) The boxes were also filled with pencil cases, grey leads, and coloured pencils of course and we love that they are also huge supporters of ours, even becoming a drop-off point for our pencils at their local branch.

Nags also went the extra mile and brought around members of his Church Group (Zion Biblical Learning Centre) to help with local community projects and helped to assemble shelves and build a huge sorting table for us as well as sorting pencils. Over two weeks a contingent of about twelve to fifteen adults and children arrived to help – it was a huge amount of fun and we cannot even begin to tell you how valuable shelving and tables are for us. It was wonderful to finally get the external support we had long wanted and the recognition and support of our local community.

In our official paperwork, we set Pencils Community up as a charity that had three core components that we agreed to have in our Constitution. They included:

1 - Advancing Education – Directly providing people of various ages and cultures from disadvantaged backgrounds, both within Australia and globally, with writing utensils, including (but not limited to) pencils, pens, textas, erasers, sharpeners, rulers and art supplies to encourage learning, growth, creativity, development, and improve their quality of life.

And...to partner with not-for-profit organisations, business, schools, individuals, and communities to provide the same pencils and stationery items to improve quality of life.

We know that all of our projects fit this element – from the children we speak to at schools who donate their supplies right through to the children we supply our pencils to – many of whom are in other countries around the world but also our local disadvantaged communities in cities and remote communities in Australia who are deprived of what we consider basic educational items and they consider a luxury.

We also know that some of our education component involves recycling and sustainability. Being able to reuse and repurpose these items gets the conversation started around waste reduction and what we can do to minimise the huge landfill problem that we have. Pencils shows a simple and yet effective model to begin tackling this modern-day issue and find practical solutions for the waste we produce.

Amazingly we continue to encourage this waste by stating that it is compulsory in many schools to have new items every year. By perpetuating a nation of wastefulness, we believe it's time to bring it back full circle. This won't happen yet, schools will not cut new stationery budgets yet, but there will be a time where this may change when many parents and teachers see the oversupply of items at the end of each school year. For now, we have an avenue for them, so we have harnessed what we can in a sustainable way for the children to reuse.

2 - Advancing social or public welfare – by arranging opportunities for people from disadvantaged backgrounds and communities to learn, grow, develop and improve their quality of life through the provision of paper, writing, and art materials.

My passion project is to see a huge increase in pencils making it to our indigenous cultures and remote communities and is a real focus for Pencils Community. We have been to many communities now in Northern Territory, Queensland and Victoria and we hope that this increases by the thousands of children we can reach and help with pencils and stationery items.

3 - Promoting reconciliation, mutual respect, and tolerance between groups of individuals that are in Australia – by working with individuals and organisations to raise awareness, raise money and fund research into mental health thereby creating an open platform for individuals to share their experiences and assist others in both managing and living with mental illness.

With the future of Lion Heart securely in good hands with the team (including me as an advisor) we can now watch it continue to evolve and grow. It will remain under the loving embrace of Pencils Community, but we agreed that Lion Heart needed to have other avenues than just 'Project Pencils'. Many people suffering with PTSD need a myriad of solutions, not just one. Later in 2018 we are looking to develop a project called 'Project Move' – where we create a weekend that involves movement.

Many people know that exercise is also beneficial for any life situation, so we liked the analogy of moving and moving forward with your life. Whether that move forward means, taking charge of your health, being a 'battle buddy' as Dion calls it, or just meeting up with someone and going for a walk or going to the gym. That move forward may even be metaphorical as you sit down with your loved ones and talk about how you have been struggling. The idea is that we have this project as an alternative project to Pencils.

The essence of Lion Heart is such that PTSD is so personal for each individual and what may work for some may not work for others. We have experts in the field such as Dion Jensen and his amazing book and PTSD programs. He has lived it and breathed it for himself personally and as ex-military and ex-police he has all the experience in the world to back him up. He also has us, his canoe fleet – of which Sarah and Lion Heart are a part, because we are a part of it. And now we have a variety of projects and plans moving forward in order to help as many of those who need help with PTSD or mental health and chronic pain. As one of our core components of Pencils Community, this was something that we were passionate about engaging in and helping those in the community.

Publicly, we state that our 'Big 3' are Education, Sustainability, and Humanitarian issues (although our Constitution incorporates these) as we believe this encapsulates what we are all about.

The pragmatic part to 'what's next?' for Pencils Community lies in what we know now and what we will learn as the year goes on.

We will continue to support our various projects, schools, and locations with items to help the children both within Australia and overseas.

We will continue to expand operations from our Ambassadors in different states in Australia and internationally and watch their projects evolve.

We hope to have a dream flight late this year where one of our Ambassadors (who happens to be a pilot), that's you Flash! Will take pencils and supplies from our Brisbane base and fly them to remote communities in Queensland to deliver. Flash is our champion to watch. He is young and hungry for change in the world. He is a passionate humanitarian and his big dreams align with ours. He will be taking a much bigger leadership role in Pencils as we move forward and grow.

Melbourne HQs will continue to expand and as we tidy up processes to make sure that we are not double-handling items and that we are getting the most pride out of what we are doing but ensuring we make quality items for our recipients.

We will continue to go out into the community at various festivals and days, visit schools, and continue to build an understanding and education of what Pencils is doing.

Health-wise, I've improved. I have taken on every radical fad (all at once) and my body has gone into some kind of WTF is this? So, I am now a gluten free, grain free, nightshade free and vegan. I can have fruit and vegetables and wine – life can be pretty solid on these ingredients alone. But it has improved my outlook and calmed down my painful joints and my eyes sight has improved so now I can look longingly at white potato chips, still a little fuzzily of course, and know that if I cave in that moment I will pay for it for a week of extra pain – and so I pretend that kale rocks my world and I simply forget now that food ever had anything that resembled enjoyment. Still, it's much better than being in agony – now it's just pain, which isn't as bad – it's all relative.

For me personally, my public speaking profile has already increased with talks and presentations at corporates, business, Rotary, and other service groups both nationally and internationally. My role is to talk about Pencils Community, from its humble beginnings to the 'boot-strapping' building of a charity. When it is your own time, money, heart and soul invested into a concept you will go further and strive harder than anyone to make it happen. There isn't a box nor pencil that hasn't gone out that I haven't had something to do with, packed, sorted, sharpened or other.

We have been able to develop programs with Rotary and in particular, have presented at the Greater Dandenong Rotary Club when a friend of ours, Terry, encouraged us to come along. We have been encouraged and supported by (them) and their wonderful donations from 'Donations-In-Kind' which included an incredible amount of first aid supplies for Tiffany and Loc Tho Orphanage in Vietnam.

A picture of Grant (my original fireman friend I thought of in the shower) roaming around this huge warehouse with an invitation to take whatever supplies he wanted for the orphanage, was priceless. We are also working with their ROMAC division this year to help create 'recovery packs' for the children who are flown in for life-threatening operations to then spend many months in hospital. We thought that these recovery packs might help them pass the time as they got better, with drawings and notes from other children inside wishing them well and a speedy recovery.

In many businesses it's easy to spend someone else's budget for something, but when it's you on the ground, making the phone calls, building the website, marketing in any way you can for $0, you know that you have to become smart and savvy in order to achieve the same results. This makes you really understand your business from the inside out and helps you to know where your gaps and shortfalls are.

We have bootstrapped our way for the last two years and learnt to be incredibly resourceful with the people who come our way and volunteer. From the mums that offer us a shed or a shelf, to the eleven-year-old who takes a box of pencils home in the school holidays to sort with friends to the people who volunteer their skills, graphic design (thank you Mariela), building our contacts, someone they know that may be able to help in some way. This community of bootstrappers are gold to us and we adore our volunteers in each and every way. They are the true 'Humanitarian Rockstars'.

We hope that with all this increased profile and brand awareness we can attract some sponsors. We don't want to become corporate, we want to keep it to a size that we remain reachable and contactable and connected to our community and our kids. We would love a warehouse to be donated and other bigger items down the track, so we can expand and grow. All for free of course! We would love to be able to offer other groups to be able to come in and participate, from disability services, the unemployed, people living with chronic pain or mental illness, seniors' activities, children's groups activities and more. The list is endless... but...

The really great thing about running a charity is that you 'live in the now'. We all know this saying but in real life it is often harder to transcend. We have daydreams and fantasies about the life we could live or have. We imagine a new house, a bigger family, a partner and a great love or romance, or we imagine the career we've always wanted. What it even feels like to be able to buy anything we want, be on holiday anywhere in the world, become a parent and achieve all those things that we may want that are just elusively out of reach at present. And then there is the 'now'.

When you run a charity such as Pencils Community your focus is on what do the kids need right now. Okay, they have a classroom with half a roof, let's give them pencils and stationery but in waterproof snap lock bags, so every time it rains they at least have half a chance of keeping their materials dry. There are children with a school and a blackboard but no chalk, okay – we have chalk how are we going to get it to these kids? And then we find a way and figure out a plan. We 'bootstrap'.

We know that many of our kids also live in the 'now'. Their futures are incredibly uncertain also. Our hope (and I guess our fantasy) is that we want them to achieve an education to improve their world, whatever that may be. To bring about some happiness, learn, grow, and develop. Ultimately, we hope it will be a systemic change and see that on the whole education levels improve in that region, that the poverty lessons and the economy booms so there are jobs for these children. But these are also our fantasies and hopes playing out.

Many of our children, despite their horrific starts in life are by nature quite happy or appear to be. They laugh and sing as they play with a ball or swim in an old bomb crater filled with water. Their very survival has focused all in on one principle and that is living in the now. We have a lot to learn from these children about creating our own happiness and it being a choice. I think this is why Pencils has worked so far. It is a charity driven by 'living in the now'. That doesn't mean we have given up on future, hope, or planning, but that it is not these aspects that drive the projects further, it's the people behind them that do. It's the Humanitarian Rockstars that do it, and they bootstrap in each and every way to achieve this. We haven't just created a charity, we have created a movement. A Pencils movement that is brought together by love and it is changing people's lives, every day.

Countries we have been to so far:

1. East Timor
2. Bali
3. Vietnam
4. Cambodia
5. Thailand
6. Indonesia
7. Sri Lanka
8. India
9. The Philippines
10. Solomon Islands
11. Papua New Guinea
12. Cook Islands
13. Fiji
14. South America (Buenos Aires)
15. Australia (Local and Remote)
16. South Africa
17. Zambia
18. Kenya
19. Uganda
20. Sierra Leone
21. New Zealand
22. Nepal
23. Malaysia
24. Samoa
25. Tonga
26. Cuba

CHAPTER 22

Transformation

Now the time has come to reflect on our journey, and just as Dion honoured the speakers that came before him, so too shall we.

I would like to honour those people who have been a part of this journey. Those who have believed and supported me on our quest to change people's lives.

I call on my 'Mountain', the physical challenges that impact me, to continually teach me to climb and rise above. As Karen Clarke would often say, 'You can't learn to climb the mountain unless it is put in front of you'.

I call on my 'River', the flow of love and energy that come from those who collect pencils, donate time, and support our endeavours, no matter how small or big that might be.

And finally, it is time to call on my 'Tribe', our Pencils Community, to continue to hold the path, and be the light to change the lives of children in need, helping them to colour their own world. We are a #Canoefleet, united in intention, effortlessly gliding towards our unified purpose.

Every story has what is called a 'Story Spine.' It is an essential part of fiction books and movies – we see it all the time. But I would say that it applies to real life also. Let me explain:

In each book or movie there is a hero, a main character. The hero lives their life until something happens to them. They go on a journey, often filled with adventure, then something may happen to cause them trauma or pain and then there is a climax to the story. They then find themselves as the hero with no other option but grow and evolve in light of this new information, and it causes them to have a massive transformation. And from then on, life as they know it is different and a new understanding leads them to live their life in a different way. It goes a little something like this:

Once Upon A Time... (there was a girl named Cindy)

Everyday... (she lived her life with her daughter)

Until something happened... (She got sick, she cleaned up her daughter's desk and had an idea, so sent out one Facebook post).

And then because of that ... (Pencils started lining up outside her door and in her letter box)

And then because of that ... (She kept Facebook posting and social media messaging. She met new people and groups)

And because of that ... (She and those who joined her, made lifelong friendships and joined together to become a united force. They sent pencils to twenty-six countries including Australia in ways you'd never dream of: container ship, car, train, bus, human, backpacks, suitcases, planes, boats, and buffalo! Thousands of children were helped with the power of the pencil!)

Until such a time.... (That we had created a huge movement of love for the pencil and all those that it helped. From volunteers to local children, to our recipient children, to our friends in business and other charities, to our Ambassadors and comrades).

And because of that... (Cindy finally understood what she had created with a simple idea, all those pencils ago when she heard it back through the eyes and mouth of people she respected immensely. #Canoefleet. She had her epiphany).

And since then... (It has changed her life and that of those close to her and those connected to the human movement of Pencils. She and her community now feel they have had a change in attitude. They display gratitude and have deeper understanding in their hearts for their own life, they value each other more and the lives of many whom they have never met, nor are they likely to meet. Their life of service is meaningful to them and to the others they can help).

The End.

But you all know that the story can't end there right? Everyone wants to know, 'but what happens next?' We are a generation of wanting more... so I'll give you a little more. Okay?

Hundreds of years ago the Italians built a train track to go over the Alps. Yet when they started the tracks, no train existed that could travel that degree of incline. They believed that it would one day happen. It was 1848 and they built a railway over the Alps from Venice to Vienna. Twenty thousand workers spent six years building what we know as the Semmering Railway track.

It was very daring for its time, with steep mountainous gradients five times what had been built in the past. But the most daring part of it all was that the railway train for it wasn't yet built, the gears for the high mountains not yet designed. However, they were strong in their belief that one day it would. And one day...it did.

The point being that it is human nature to want to have faith and belief. We see it around the world today in every country and culture we live in. Human beings are designed to be good, joyous, curious, and creative. They have an innate desire to be close to others and share experiences and life's moments with them. It doesn't have to be religious; it can be scientific also. What is essential though is that we all carry this wish, faith, belief, or hope.

We want for this and it is what makes our hearts sing and our faces smile.

I have learnt that in Pencils Community or in fact in life, people come and go, some friends, some partners. You can't take this personally, you must continue to walk your own path for you. Sometimes you compromise, other times you feel compromised in yourself, but you must keep walking and never give up, even if at the time it hurts your heart. *Know thy self.* You must learn to be grateful for their help when they could and respect that they too have their own journeys and paths to walk. You will be able to take lessons from each experience and continue to grow in yourself. There will be others that walk with you at some point too. Those 'others' may stay the course and your relationships deepen and friendships strengthen. And then there are people that will always walk with you in your life and 'stay the course'.

I learnt hard lessons early on about myself and others. I learnt that you have to stay strong and true to the course, to being *yourself.* I have set Pencils Community up as a legacy, as something I can pass on to my daughter. I don't have any assets or anything monetary to give to her at this point and this is what I can give her; I can give her a model of a charity that incorporates generosity and giving. It will also teach her life lessons and business lessons and it is filled with amazing role models and support, should she come off course along the way. Pencils will always be passed onto her to manage and all the children and recipients are my beneficiaries.

I can show Olive that no matter what life challenges you face you can overcome anything. *Know thy ledge.* No excuses. She will learn that from me. I can already see her young humanitarian ways as she stands in front of other kids and shares with them the Pencils story.

I hope that she says, 'Stuff it Mum, I want to go backpacking with my girlfriends in Europe,' and all I can say is 'good'. My first and foremost job is a mother preparing her as best as I can for life. Showing her as long as she has compassion and respect for herself, she can create any path she likes; it doesn't have to be a traditional one. I know that there will be people to guide her and people on the board and around to make sure Pencils continues as it should, I just hope she employs someone great while she is off gallivanting around the world!

I know I don't have much, but I do know that what I do have to pass down to her is something that can never be bought.

Life is never predictable – it never follows the list we make when we are younger. It changes you in so many ways as it takes you on twists and turns, almost as if it has its own adventure for you planned.

When I first came up with the idea of Pencils Community two years ago, it was a beautiful and simple idea that just made sense.

'What's your vision?' they asked.

'What is your strategy?' they enquired.

'They' being the collective community.

Their response would then be littered with how to be successful, what the success principles are and what I would need to do to create success. It fell on deaf ears, I wasn't in that space and it wasn't what I wanted to hear. It was my *belief* that Pencils would evolve and grow into exactly what it needed to be.

Two years later, I was asked the same question.

'What are you doing with your strategy this year?' to become successful.

I smiled, already knowing my answer.

My response was meant with warmth, it came from my core, a deep inner place of knowing and belief. It came from my pure gut instinct that I know operate on and it felt exactly right.

'Pencils Community is already successful,' I said with my eyes shining and my heart full of joy.

We help thousands of children colour their life. We colour it with hope and opportunity and erase helplessness and hopelessness. We have already succeeded in our mission. Will we continue to change children's lives with more pencils and more communication about Pencils? Of course, we will! But, I only need look into the eyes of any of the children that we have helped, and I know instantly that my heart sings and my face smiles and so too do theirs.

I listen to my daughter talk about Pencils Community with her 9-year-old friends on the bed in her bedroom. Tucked up in mermaid blankets, legs crossed as they talk amongst each other. They are not talking just about makeup, Minecraft or whatever their latest fad is; intermingled into their conversation is a deep understanding of helping others, making a difference and saving the world by helping children who in their own words, 'they are just like us.'

That's the success I am looking for and I already have it, we as a community, a Pencils Community already have it. Why? Because it comes from a place of love.

I was focused on a quest to leave a legacy. To question and evaluate why we are put on this earth. To help others through service and love, and in doing so I have found a deeper love for myself and my family.

My Pencils Community family.

The End.

Still not enough? Want more? Okay, okay....

We want to get a huge warehouse with see-through walls, one area where we can have our sorting and workshops, have children and school groups come through and sort and learn. And on the other side we would love an art gallery with the children's work in it. With all sales going back to the children's family and village. We would love a little coffee shop, gluten free, vegan, of course and we would love to have planted our 'Pencils Forest' out the back so that we can replace the trees and environment that are used to make the pencils that are made somewhere far away, but we can all do our bit right.

We want to drive around in a Pencils vehicle being able to collect the pencils and the kids recognise our van. Then we would like one in every state. With t-shirts for all our Ambassadors to wear as they drive around their local areas. We will, as always, focus on Education, Sustainability and Humanitarian issues, visit schools and teach them about Pencils and what they can do to help. And after we do this we will create more dreams and be curious about new ways in which we can help.

And we will continue to do this after I am long gone. To know one's purpose in life is to ignite one's passion. It is a legacy already as the torch passes from one person to the next. This is the essence that is never forgotten as it is passed on to future generations, because it is found within – it is inside of all of us already.

The End...or really...it's never the end.

Do you feel now that you have what it takes to be a HUMANITARIAN ROCKSTAR? To find your #Canoefleet and start your journey?

I know you do...And you already know this too. So, let's get started today, shall we? *One day*? No, I don't believe so...**Day one**!

Now it's your turn Humanitarian Rockstar.

On **YOUR** mark...

Get Set...

GO!

How can you help Pencils Community?

There are so many kids out there who need your support, and all it takes is the simple act of giving! Now is the time to step up, and here at Pencils Community, we've made it easy:

- VOLUNTEER your time; VOLUNTEER your ideas; and VOLUNTEER your effort! All these good things help build a better world for us, and a brighter future for our children.
- Spread the WORD! Be part of this positive social movement. We're all over Facebook; find us, share us, like us and tag us. We'd love to hear from you.
- DONATE pencils and help in the packing, sorting and distributing to those in need. Our volunteers even take pencils on holidays, gifting them to nearby children in need!
- Offer warehouse SPACE! We'd love to partner with you and promote your engagement with those in need. It's as easy as clearing a few shelves for some pencils.
- Offer logistic SUPPORT! All it takes is a car and some space. Even better if you have a bus, a truck or a company, to get pencils where they're needed most! And if you're in the business of moving, we're always in need of new and practical ideas.
- FUNDRAISE! If you're a bright spark with fresh ideas on raising money for children in need, we'd love to hear from you!
- CELEBRITY Endorsement! If you're famous, like us, we want you on board. Use your fame for good, not evil (kidding). We're a social movement and we help thousands of children every year. A bit of influence goes a long way in creating positive and lasting change.
- SPONSORSHIPS and Grants! Got advice, knowledge and the want to make a change? You could help us more than you think!
- Joint VENTURES! Don't be shy, get your business involved. Improve workplace engagement, professional development and staff enthusiasm by giving back to the community. It's also great for your broader image.

Whoever you are, whatever you do, it only takes one pencil, and we'd love to hear from you! Step up, join the social movement and build a brighter future for our children; one pencil at a time.

Acknowledgements

I want to thank the humble pencil, small in size but not in stature.

For giving the chance to millions of people around the world to learn, create, develop, and grow.

Thank you for being the opportunity and hope that they need.

Thank you for helping our children be who they want to be and helping them to leave their 'mark' on the world.

-Cindy xx

Charity/Community Contacts

Pencils Community
Pencils Community Email: info@pencilscommunity.com
Phone: +61 437 094 049
Website: www.pencilscommunity.com
Facebook: 'Pencils Community'
Instagram: 'Pencils Community'
Twitter: @pencilscomm

Cindy Rochstein (Founder)
Website: www.cindyrochstein.com
Website: www.emagineacademy.com
LinkedIn: 'in.cindyrochstein'

Lion Heart
Website: www.Lion Heartcouragetothrive.com
Facebook: 'LION HEART Courage'

Ocean Reeve
Ocean Reeve Email: info@oceanreeve.com
Phone: +61 415 438 534
Website: www.oceanreeve.com
Website: www.emagineacademy.com
Facebook: 'Ocean Reeve'
LinkedIn: 'Ocean Reeve'

Dion Jensen
Website: www.dionjensen.com
Website: www.successforsoldiers.com

Agent:

Ocean Reeve Email: info@oceanreeve.com
Phone: +61 415 438 534
Website: www.oceanreeve.com
Website: www.emagineacademy.com
Facebook: 'Ocean Reeve'
LinkedIn: 'Ocean Reeve'

Jason Smith
Ocean Reeve Email: info@oceanreeve.com
Phone: +61 415 438 534
Website: www.oceanreeve.com
Website: www.emagineacademy.com

Karen Clarke
Karen Clarke Email: karen@frombulliedtobrilliant.com
Website: www.frombulliedtobrilliant.com
Website: www.emagineacademy.com
Facebook: 'Ocean Reeve'

Case Studies

- Jaime Ramos (SANCSS) http://www.sancss.org.au/
- Facebook: https://www.facebook.com/Sancss/
- Michael Gallus (Footys4All) http://www.footys4all.com.au/
- Facebook: https://www.facebook.com/Footys4All/
- Bela Mitchell (OrphFund) (http://www.orphfund.org/)
- Facebook: https://www.facebook.com/orphfund/
- Michelle Euniton (Colour My Story)
- Facebook: https://www.facebook.com/colourourstory/
- Tiffany Pham (Loc Tho Orphanage)
  Email: Phamilyfoundation@gmail.com
- Karla Eyre (Friends of Brilliant Star – Solomon Islands)
- http://friendsofbrilliantstar.com/
- Facebook: https://www.facebook.com/groups/270999640037033/

All our Volunteers

All our Ambassadors

All our Junior Volunteers

Specifically referenced:

- Mason Howard, Pascoe Vale North Primary School
- Madeline Baker, Mt Eliza Primary School
- Abigail Brown, Mentone Girls' Grammar School
- Ada Jenkins, Mentone Girls' Grammar School
- Reine Clemow (Acquira Wealth Partners)
  Email: reine@acquirawp.com.au
- Mike Harvey – (On Your Side Investments)
  Email: mike@onyourside.consulting

- Bunnings (Carrum Downs, Victoria)
  https://www.bunnings.com.au/stores/vic/carrum-downs?utm_source=google&utm_medium=places&utm_content=bunnings-carrum-downs&utm_campaign=googleplaces
- Commonwealth Bank (Seaford Branch, Victoria)
  https://www.commbank.com.au/personal/locate-us/vic/seaford/063492.html

References

Articles & Information:

http://www.observer.ug/news-headlines/43265-two-killed-in-kasese-police-post-attack

http://www.monitor.co.ug/News/National/Policeman-killed-in-latest-Kasese-attacks/688334-3132142-ampq4dz/index.html

http://business.inquirer.net/168288/what-the-church-of-jesus-christ-of-lds-did-for-the-visayas#ixzz572ZTUtQk

https://www.mercycorps.org/articles/philippines/quick-facts-what-you-need-know-about-super-typhoon-haiyan

https://www.google.com.au/search?q=beyonce+song+i+was+here+lyrics&rlz=1C1NHXL_enAU762AU762&oq=beyonce+&aqs=chrome.1.69i57j35i39j0l4.3150j0j7&sourceid=chrome&ie=UTF-8

http://www.songfacts.com/detail.php?id=23334

https://www.youtube.com/watch?v=-LbEnH6Lqbo

http://www.sciencemag.org/news/2017/12/lower-your-social-class-wiser-you-are-suggests-new-study

https://www.youtube.com/playlist?list=PLRRTHFFklAxk8bJMIgWZamX-GiqYsqcU

www.google.com

www.etymonline.com/word/knowledge

www.mindfulnext.org

https://www.jencompton.com/lifes-a-mango/